THE DECONVERTED MAN

A GUIDE TO HAPPINESS, FREEDOM, AND PURPOSE AFTER LEAVING FUNDAMENTALIST RELIGION

CHASE AUSTIN

Copyright © 2020 by Chase Austin

All rights reserved.

No part of this book may be reproduced in any form or by any electronic or mechanical means, including information storage and retrieval systems, without written permission from the author, except for the use of brief quotations in a book review.

Cover art by The Cover Collection

THE DECONVERTED MAN

CONTENTS

Introduction   vii

PART I
1. My Story   3
2. The Two Paths   12
3. Your Happiness   21
4. The Seven Life Areas   35

PART II
5. Your Money   51
6. Your Health   89
7. Your Family   109
8. Your Social Life   127
9. Your Hobbies   144
10. Your Relationships With Women   158
11. Your Spirituality   190

PART III
12. Your Life   215
13. Your Mission   224
14. Your Decision   241

About the Author   249
Notes   251

INTRODUCTION

When a man deconverts from his fundamentalist religion, it's usually regarded as a pivotal moment in that man's life—one in which he's finally found true freedom and joy.

But is it really? Far more often, it seems that deconversion is followed by loss, depression, and emptiness. A man's life made complete sense when it was dedicated to God. But now, in the absence of someone to serve and worship, he doesn't know what to do or who to be.

People still in the fold of fundamentalism will nod their heads and tell him, "That's what you get for not believing in God anymore." But the deconverted man can't believe in God again even if he wanted to. The evidence and arguments for the existence of a Creator no longer make sense to him, so he is forced to choose new truths over old comforts.

However, those truths feel bleak and empty.

I'd been trying for a long time to put my finger on this. Does the proposition that we are the product of random evolution, live only once, and disappear when we die mean that we should feel hollow and depressed all the time? Of course not. Yet that is still how a lot of deconverted men live today.

I reached out to a good friend of mine with these thoughts. He summarized years of contemplation into one succinct quote:

"One of the great failures of the 'non-belief' movement is adequately presenting alternatives. Secular Humanism works as an ethical approach, but there's a hole where purpose and meaning used to be. It's like they seek to deconvert and then just… leave it."

Bullseye.

Think back to your old church. When the pastor or priest gave an especially moving sermon on Sunday morning and someone was "saved" as a result, what did they do next? They followed up with this person. A longtime believer sat down with him and answered his questions, told him what came next in his faith journey, and then plugged him into a small group where he could be discipled by a mentor.

Now consider non-believers. They evangelize their truths the same way churches do, only they seek to pull people in the opposite direction of faith. Instead of the Bible, they use science, logic, and reason to convince their prospect that God does not exist. When that prospect declares, "You're right! I no longer believe in God," what does the non-believing evangelist do next?

Nothing.

In his mind, he's saved a soul from the box of religion and his job is done. Unfortunately, the deconverted person is now left to their own devices to figure out what comes next in a post-fundamentalism world.

Introduction

Wrenching someone from his fundamentalist religion, especially if they have spent significant time in that belief system and lifestyle, is a traumatic experience. His entire way of life and expectations for his future have now been exposed as a lie. This newly-deconverted man—now without meaning, purpose, or direction—is left alone to navigate a world that is brand new and mysterious. This often leads to disastrous results.

These souls returning to the real world are tragically "caught and released" into the wild at their most vulnerable moment. It should be no surprise, then, that so many deconverted men still feel lost after leaving their religion.

But it doesn't have to be this way.

This book is written to meet men at this transitional moment and show them how to rediscover what life means after their deconversion.

Defining Fundamentalism

In this book, I use the word "fundamentalism" as an umbrella term for the beliefs, teachings, and lifestyles that are found in the Church.

For my purposes, fundamentalism describes any Bible adhering Christian community that believes in traditional Christian dogma—the existence of God, the inerrancy of Scripture, the resurrection of Jesus, and that professing faith in Jesus Christ is the only path to salvation and an eternity in heaven. These communities also believe that rejecting the established dogma results in an individual suffering eternal punishment after they die, usually in a physical place called hell.

Some moderate and liberal Christians may try to

Introduction

shake off the term "fundamentalist" by saying it only describes relatively small and fringe groups that are extreme in their beliefs, behaviors, and actions. They point to churches like Westboro Baptist Church—the very conservative church that made headlines by protesting the funerals of soldiers—as one such extreme example, then rationalize that "real Christians" don't do these terrible things and are therefore not fundamentalists. They typically prefer terms such as evangelicalism.

However, since moderate and liberal church communities still believe in the same traditional Christian dogma, I still consider them fundamentalists.

Fundamentalism, for the purposes of this book, can also include other Christian-adjacent or non-Christian sects, groups, and religions. Examples would be Catholics, Mormons, Jehovah's Witnesses, Christian Scientists, and Scientologists, just to name a few.

I'll also use the word Church with a capital "C" to denote the all-encompassing body of churches that profess and teach traditional Christian dogma and the cultures and lifestyles that are found in their congregations. It matters little what specific church you went to or what denomination you considered yourself. If you spent any significant amount of time in Church culture, you know what it entails—Sunday school, youth group, praise and worship, mission trips (short and long-term) service projects, weekend retreats, Bible camp, Vacation Bible School, Bible studies, discipleship, evangelizing, and many more activities and events that occurred within the framework of what I mentioned before—the dogma of a fundamentalist belief system.

Introduction

Why Men?

You may be wondering why is this book speaking only to men. After all, there are plenty of deconverted women out there, too.

The answer: Because I'm a man, and that's who I feel qualified to speak to. We all share the human experience, but men and women are different in many key ways. And when it comes to talking about practical approaches to life in the middle of a traumatic deconversion experience, I feel it's best to take gender into consideration. Men and women are equal, obviously, but they tend to view and approach life in unique ways.

For example and generally speaking, men and women seem to handle pain differently. They handle discomfort differently. They handle trauma differently. They seek happiness in different ways and in different things.

All of that is fine. Neither is better than the other. But for the sake of clarity and specificity, I have chosen to focus on men.

That being said, women are more than welcome to read along with us, and I encourage them to do so! If you're a woman and have a male spouse, partner, or friend who has deconverted, this book can help you understand what he may be going through and how he can realistically and practically move forward if he's feeling stuck. And if you found this book before he did, please loan him your copy or give it as a gift.

Another point: This book is extremely "pro-man" but not "anti-woman." If you're someone—man or woman—who thinks that enthusiastically supporting men automatically makes that person anti-women, this book probably isn't for you.

Also, for the sake of simplicity and to keep the text manageable and readable, topics regarding sex, dating, marriage, and relationships have been written with a man-woman framework simply because that is my personal experience and what I feel most qualified to speak on.

However, I strongly affirm LGTBQ+ individuals—especially those finding acceptance in the LGTBQ+ community after leaving the Church. Although I am using the man-woman framework in this book, I am trusting that the readers who don't adhere to that structure in their personal lives to make the necessary connections to their own circumstances.

So now that the housekeeping is out of the way, I will take my reasoning a bit further.

What this Book Is About

Scores of books, breaking news stories, documentaries, podcasts, YouTube channels, and websites have exposed many of the horrific things that the Church has wrought throughout its history up until today. I'm talking about sexual abuse, emotional abuse, gaslighting, financial corruption, scams, pedophilia, persecution of same-sex couples, and more. You've probably already heard or read about much of this. One or more of them may be why you decided to deconvert in the first place.

This book will not address these topics. There are plenty of others that cover these travesties much better than this one can. Rather, this book is about how

Introduction

damaging aspects of life in the Church seep in through the cracks and invade our subconscious minds and continue to dictate our actions even after we deconvert. Often, the remnants of these belief patterns remain long after we think we've successfully cleared out the baggage.

The Church has taken considerable control of our money, our health, our families, our social lives, our hobbies, our relationships with women, and our spiritual lives, often in ways that we still don't realize, even years after deconversion.

It's easy to point your finger at the megachurch pastor caught with his secretary and declare, "You were wrong to do that," but it's less obvious to turn your attention inward and analyze the nuances of your own life that the Church's false teachings still pervade.

This book was written to expose these smaller cracks and crevices and help you to clear them out.

I will address "you" throughout this book, but also keep in mind that I am also speaking to myself because I am on this journey with you, brother. Also, many of my conclusions were learned the hard way, and I'd like you to avoid the same pitfalls that ensnared me.

I also use the word "journey" because that's exactly what we're all on. The topics I discuss in the following pages could very well take an entire lifetime to address. That's okay. I firmly believe it's work well worth doing, and that we will all be better off in the end.

Overview

This book is organized into three parts:

- Part 1 establishes my premise and lays the foundation for the practical applications that come later in the book.
- Part 2 addresses the seven key areas that make up a complete life.
- Part 3 puts all of these pieces together into a plan for moving forward into a meaningful post-deconversion life.

Part 1

Spoiler alert: I believe that your overall happiness comes from your ability to live freely and autonomously—something you were never allowed to do within the confines of the Church. If that sounds selfish to you, I suspect that you still have some church teachings to clear out of your system. Usually, the only person telling you that you aren't allowed to be happy is yourself.

You may say, "But I'm happy with what I have."

I would challenge you to read further and take another look at your life. Are you truly happy or are you just getting by? Do you have more than a few "bad days" a month or are most of your days good with random bits of bad in between?

Worst of all, do you think any of those scenarios are the best you can hope for?

Even if your church didn't explicitly say so (most of them do, though), it taught that you should be satisfied with what God has given you. If you aren't, then you need to work on your heart. This is a dangerous teaching that has caused many men to settle for lives that happen to fall into their laps and assume it's "God's will."

Introduction

Now that you know that God isn't real, you should realize that what fell into your lap by chance is only that—a product of merely going with the flow. You no longer need to feel "thankful" for it if you can honestly say to yourself that you want more. This book will help you to realize this.

Part 2

A man's life is composed of seven distinct (but sometimes overlapping) areas:

1. Your money.
2. Your health.
3. Your family.
4. Your social life.
5. Your hobbies.
6. Your relationships with women.
7. Your spirituality.

How many of them do you feel satisfied with? How well are they working?

In addition to the influence of the Church's traditional theology, I've noticed that these areas of our lives have also been indoctrinated by other more subtle beliefs. Over the years, we've unconsciously absorbed a lot of information from being in the Church that is simply wrong. That information still negatively impacts our post-deconversion lives.

Skim that list again and consider how truly happy you would be if all of those areas were awesome instead of "meh." So in this section, we will tackle each of those areas in depth, expose to you what the Church taught (directly or indirectly) about each, and show how you can regain control of each area in a real-world context.

Part 3

This final section ties everything together and shows you how to take all that you learned in the previous section and incorporate it into your life with intentional action. It's the altar call, if you will—the decision to change your life.

This section also addresses one of the biggest problems deconverted men face: the loss of purpose and a sense of meaning. The penultimate chapter—possibly the most important in the book—will walk you through how to find meaning again, step-by-step, after losing it in your deconversion.

PART I

Chapter 1
MY STORY

"By three methods we may learn wisdom: First, by reflection, which is noblest; Second, by imitation, which is easiest; and third by experience, which is the bitterest." — Confucius

This book isn't about me. It's about you. Nevertheless, you may be wondering who I am and why I care so much about the issues I'm addressing. What follows is a very brief overview of my life within the Church and ultimately how I left, why I left, and where I am today.

Childhood

I was exposed to the Church my entire life and was a constant Sunday school attendee. Those classes were taught by elderly church volunteers who earnestly believed they were doing the right thing by investing in the lives of the church community's young people.

I was never skeptical. I had no reason to believe that

the adults in my life would lie to me. I viewed my Sunday school teachers the same way as my teachers at school—they were to be trusted, respected, and they were always right.

One year, at the St. Patrick's Day parade that happens annually in my town, some man handed me a booklet. He never spoke to me. I didn't know what it was and didn't even look at it but decided to keep it. I don't remember showing it to anyone.

I read it later that night. In a comic book style, it explained that if you did bad things, such as not paying attention during church, God would not see your name in the book of life when you die and you would go straight to hell. But if you prayed, did good things, and went to church, you went to heaven.

I put the booklet in the bottom drawer of my dresser —not especially hidden—and would refer to it many times over the years. It had more influence on me than I realized at the time. It had a huge impact on my thinking.

I know for a fact I still have it somewhere and I'll probably never throw it away.

Young Adult Years

I was saved at the age of eleven at a week-long summer church camp. It happened at the predictable moment—the final night, when the music is cranked a little louder and the speaker is more emotional and insistent than in his previous messages. The jokes are gone. It's all business.

With artificially created emotions running high, I was

manipulated into accepting Jesus Christ as my Lord and Savior.

Throughout middle school and high school, I navigated the waters of a life in the Church with both successes and failures. I would ride a spiritual high for a while which would inevitably be followed by a spiritual low. A church weekend retreat or a particularly good youth group sermon would lift me out of the dumps and ignite me for several weeks. Then I would crash. The cycle continued and I never thought much of it.

I was a good kid. I never got into much trouble, mostly because I didn't want to sin. I took that very seriously, even at a young age. God gave commands and I had to obey them.

In some of my worst moments, I became "holier than thou" because of my ability to obey God's commands. In reality, I was just a boring teenager too afraid to get his hands dirty.

In my senior year of high school, I decided that I was mature enough to take my faith more seriously. All of the previous years had been a back-and-forth roller coaster ride that couldn't possibly be acceptable in the eyes of God. I had to double down and be more consistent with my faith.

College Years

In 2006, at the beginning of my freshman year of college, I joined the university campus church and began volunteering in their youth ministry since youth group had had the biggest impact on me growing up. Even today, I can say that it was a rewarding experience. The kids I watched grow over the years were outstanding young men—far more intelligent and wiser than I ever was at their age.

During my time with the youth ministry, I sincerely wanted to grow spiritually. I sought out a mentor and we met once a week to talk deeply on topics such as the Bible, God, and what it meant to be a Christian and a disciple.

I don't remember exactly when it clicked, but I realized I wasn't okay with being discipled while having not read the entire Bible. It was the crux of the religion that I'd based my life on.

That's right, I was one of those Christians who hadn't read the Bible. I never claimed to have read the whole thing, but I did convince myself that I'd read most of it. I counted the scriptures that were read in sermons, and because of the sheer number of sermons I'd heard, I had always considered myself as having almost read the entire New Testament.

So one day, firm in my new resolution, I sat down with my Bible and started at the place that seemed the most obvious to me—the beginning.

In that first sitting, I read through the first chapter of Genesis. The creation story. Adam and Eve. I'd heard it referenced hundreds of times while growing up in the Church. But a thought popped into my head, completely unbidden and seemingly from out of nowhere. It was this:

If you asked a man who lived ten thousand years ago to describe where he thought the world came from, of course he would write something like this.

I felt blasphemous. I felt dirty. It lingered in my mind. It didn't go away, even though I desperately wanted it to.

Also, right there in that same story, I was forced to

ponder another matter: That the entire Christian faith was divided on what to think about those two short chapters. One group thought it was literally true that the earth was only six-thousand-years old despite what science had uncovered. The other group believed that the creation story wasn't entirely literal.

I had to decide. If I was going to be strong in my faith, I needed to know what I believed.

I chose the comfortable combination of science and faith. My personality and brain just couldn't be forced to ignore the fossils, history, and carbon dating. But that decision led me to another problem. If that creation story —the very first few chapters of the Bible—weren't considered to be literal, what else in the Bible was metaphorical?

Left with these questions, I completed my goal and read the entire Bible. It took me the better part of a year. Some if it was pleasantly entertaining, like the book of Joshua. Other books were a slog, such as Leviticus. But as I read, I never forgot my initial reaction—that perhaps not all of this was literal history.

I also read *about* the Bible as I went. I quickly discovered a new liberal Christian school of thought that felt the same way about the Bible as I did: that it was more metaphorical than fact. What I came to realize was that as long as Jesus died and rose from the dead, nothing else in the Bible needed to be literal. But if Jesus hadn't risen on the third day, the entire religion was rendered moot.

Around age 23, I started listening to the "Unbelievable" podcast, a British radio program that brought together believers and nonbelievers for friendly debates. I ravenously binged through the back catalogue, soaking up the information and points on both sides. I horrified myself when I realized that the atheist guest almost always made more sense to me. I felt my resolve slipping. So I did what I probably shouldn't have—shelve the turmoil into the back of my brain and bury it deep.

A deconversion just wasn't something I felt ready to deal with.

Then, in 2013, I took a 15-week "Perspectives" class, a course that teaches Christians how to do mission work and why it's so important. It was a sharp departure from the emotion-based mission work where all you do is hug orphans in developing countries. This was real missionary work. You were either in or out. No short-termers accepted.

The class reinterpreted the entire Christian faith in a way that made total sense to my pragmatic mind. It removed all the focus on the high emotions I'd grown tired of in normal church services and turned the faith into a logical progression of evangelizing the entire world. It demonstrated with maps, statistics, and stories of historical missionaries how the world was truly won over for God.

It made so much sense at the time. Finally, the mission of God presented as it really was: a mission. There was work to be done!

That class nearly saved my faith.

Moving Away

When I was 26 years old, I moved from the United States to the Middle East for work. I relocated to an area that was religiously tolerant but I also knew it would be nothing like the Bible Belt in which I grew up. Further, I would no longer be surrounded by people who had spent their entire lives in the Church.

The church always talked about how important it was to have a community. But I sometimes wondered if that directive was designed to keep members from getting a peek at the other side of the veil. By leaving a deep-rooted church community, I was going to get that peek. If I still retained my old beliefs, then I knew that my faith was rock solid. If my faith was supposed to last, this move would be the ultimate test.

During my years spent living and working in the Middle East, I lived without God. It wasn't an intentional decision. It just kind of happened as I lived my life. It's not that I went on a sinful rampage, but I had stopped praying, stopped having quiet times, stopped attending church, and no longer read my Bible.

And nothing terrible happened. My life didn't collapse. My mood didn't deteriorate. God didn't punish me. Instead, I conducted my life in a way that felt natural to me. For the first time, I spent considerable time with people the Church had always told me were wrong: Atheists, Muslims, same-sex couples, and people who weren't conservative in their politics.

And they were all quite pleasant and normal.

Also, being in the Middle East revealed to me how much a person's religion is influenced by where they were born in the world. It should come as no surprise that the people of a country that technically makes it illegal to not adhere to Islam is full of Muslims. Likewise, I was born in the U.S. Bible Belt so it's no great surprise that I became an evangelical Christian.

It was during these years of "living without God" that I

realized how much the teachings of the Church and Church culture still influenced my thoughts and behaviors. They were holding me back from living the life I'd always known I wanted. Over time, I analyzed those thoughts and behaviors and worked to remove them from my patterns of thinking and acting. It was hard work but my life improved dramatically, all without God. The details of the changes I made are the subject of the next section of this book.

Once I had improved my life without the help of prayer and faith, I felt more comfortable thinking about the fact that I no longer believed. Still, I tried to postpone an "official declaration" for as long as possible. I felt that once it was made, there was no going back. The genie never goes back into the bottle. Honestly, I was afraid.

In the end, however, I could no longer live in a way that wasn't true to how I really thought and felt. I couldn't spend any more time in a wishy-washy state of doubt and uncertainty. When I finally began to consider myself a deconverted man, there was never a flashy, dramatic moment. I never made a public announcement. I simply spent time in quiet contemplation and accepted the fact that I no longer believed.

Your Story

That's enough about me, because again, this book is about you.

I love a good deconversion story. They're addicting. I always try to guess the storyteller's tipping point. Did they have one too many unanswered prayers? Did they try to perform miracle healings that never worked? Or was it similar to my story in that they found the historicity of the Bible to be unreliable?

But as I listened to more and more of these deconversion stories, I also heard about the negatives, the fallout. There was confusion, heartbreak, and trauma. Many of these stories had no real ending. The person was still wondering which way to go now that religion had failed them.

Through a massive amount of trial and error (usually error), I compiled an effective and practical way to remove the damaging religious clutter that still polluted my brain after my faith started slipping and build a life that was true to who I was outside the Church.

I knew I couldn't keep it all to myself. If I found it valuable, then other people would as well.

Chapter 2

THE TWO PATHS

"Even if you're on the right track, you'll get run over if you just sit there." — Will Rogers

Following deconversion, there are two main paths that most men tend to go down. Both lead to unhappiness. Both leave men confused as to why they are still struggling after deciding they no longer believe in God. The two paths represent two archetypes of deconverted men: the Angry Bitter Atheist (ABA) and the Traumatized Empty Shell (TES).

The Angry Bitter Atheist (ABA)

Let me introduce you to Jason. Actually, you probably already know him. There's a "Jason" who has left every church in the world. Maybe you're like Jason.

Jason has spent his entire life as a fundamentalist, evangelical Christian. Then one day, while Jason is doing his quiet time, he comes across a story in the Bible that is told twice but with different sets of details in each. They can't both be right. That doesn't make any sense to him. He believes the Bible to be the inerrant word of God. Could it be that he's found a mistake?

Jason asks his pastor, who tells him to have faith. Usually Jason does have faith, but he's a bit older now and this time that answer isn't good enough. So he researches the apparent contradiction and discovers quite easily using the power of the internet that he is not the first person to realize this Biblical error. In fact, it is just one of hundreds more on a list.

Thus begins the slippery slope.

Up until now, Jason had only read the Bible, C.S. Lewis, and Francis Chan among a few others, but those were his favorites. Now he's discovered Richard Dawkins, Christopher Hitchens, Bart Ehrman, and Sam Harris. That slippery slope just got a lot steeper.

A few months later, Jason deconverts and becomes an atheist. He can no longer reconcile the nonsensical claims of the Bible and the Church.

He now considers himself open-minded for the first time in his life and has no qualms about reading atheist material that, to him, was previously forbidden. He gets a feel-good dopamine hit every time he turns one of those pages. It's a similar thrill to doing something naughty or rebelling against authority. Since God no longer exists to Jason, he's getting away with it.

He feels his brain expanding with new knowledge— knowledge that he regrets was always right in front of him but overlooked because he was blinded by faith.

Like most people who binge on Netflix shows, Jason binges on science, evolution, the Big Bang theory, the historical view of the Bible, and the archaeological record. It all makes so much sense to him now. He laments that all the "mysteries of God" the Church relied on for defining its specialness could easily be solved by removing God from the equation.

The world, it turns out, is actually quite predictable and sensible when it follows the laws of physics and evolution. Somewhere during his spiritual development, Jason somehow missed out on the "secrets" which weren't ever really secrets.

For all these reasons, he's *angry*. And rightfully so. It's this *anger* that drives Jason forward. What does he do next?

Just as Jason once fervently evangelized the Gospel, he now feels he must evangelize his new truth. If he was wrong the entire time he was a believer, then so was everyone else. He begins by announcing his deconversion to his friends, family, and church. As predicted, he is met with shock, horror, pity, and some outrage. Deep down, Jason revels in the shockwaves he's sent through his former religious community. It's like agitating an ant hill.

He can't comprehend how the people in the Church won't even consider the new truths he's found. Whether consciously or not, Jason determines himself intellectually superior, or at least more open-minded, and begins to look down his nose at his previous religious community. This path of perceived superiority carries over into internet forums, both religious and non-religious. Jason makes posts that are provocative and anti-religion. Almost always, someone bites, and the two engage in a debate that no one wins.

The church members closest to Jason set up lunch

meetings to hear his story and to offer him advice and prayer. Jason meets with these people because he delights in proving them wrong. After all, he's armed with an arsenal of facts, science, and history. Over time, these friends give up on Jason. They say they'll keep him in their prayers, but that is still effectively giving up. Jason's anger keeps him distant and closed off. He wants nothing to do with anyone—even longtime friends—who remains in the faith.

Furthermore, the non-believers on Jason's social media grow tired of his constant baiting for debates and ranting about religion. They are happy that Jason has finally seen the light but grow frustrated because he can't seem to move on and ignore religion like they've been doing for most of their lives. These non-believers start distancing themselves from Jason as well.

Jason wakes up one day and realizes there is nothing left. He's shunned his old church community and annoyed everyone else. He spends his spare time angry, brooding over social media and online forums and exchanging messages with other angry, recently-deconverted people. He blames God, religion, and the Church for wasting his life and time. In especially dark moments, he feels that his life is meaningless due to the absence of an afterlife.

This is the Angry Bitter Atheist (ABA): someone who has spent too long in the anger phase of deconversion to the point that it's negatively impacting their lives or prevents them from improving their lives and going forward. It's okay to be angry when you first deconvert, but it's in your best interest to begin improving your post-fundamentalist life as fast as possible. You have a lot of lost time to make up for.

The ABA is an easy trap to fall into but must be avoided. You just end up trading one strict dogma (fundamentalism) for another (Hitchens-esque atheism). All that posting and debating is its own type of evangelism. When you were a Christian, you were hell-bent on spreading the good news. As an ABA, you are hell-bent on spreading the bad news.

True freedom from religion means moving on. Take your time to be angry—it's part of the grieving process—but don't dwell there, and don't bring others into it. Anger and hate breeds more of the same, so you need to break out of the cycle.

The Traumatized Empty Shell (TES)

Let me introduce you to Michael. Actually, I don't need to introduce you because you already know him. Like Jason, a "Michael" has left every church in the world. Maybe you're just like Michael.

Michael has been a fundamentalist Christian his entire life. He grew up in the church, never missed Sunday school or youth group, went to a Christian high school, and has gone on several mission trips. He's had personal experiences that he believes to be from God.

Michael believes that he is worthless without God. He believes the Bible when it says his good deeds are like "filthy rags." He has been taught this repeatedly throughout his many years in the church, usually subtly but sometimes explicitly. As such, he wants to be less like himself and more like Jesus. He prays for Jesus to take away the parts of him that are "unworthy" and replace them with Christ-like behaviors.

Michael also believes his sexuality is bad, so he prays away his desires. He almost conquers his lustful sin.

Michael believes money changes people for the worse, so he never pursues it. What little money he does have, he tithes every week.

Michael avoids engaging in hobbies. He believes they only distract from his prayer and evangelism.

Michael never hangs out with any other guys he knows because he does not consider them up to his strict standards. Michael fears they may be a bad influence on him.

Michael is continuously praised for the sacrifices he makes for Jesus. He is held in high esteem by his pastors and presented as a poster child for the church—a demonstration of what true, dedicated faith should look like.

Then one day, while Michael is doing his quiet time, he comes across a story in the Bible that is told twice but with different sets of details in each. They can't both be right. That doesn't make any sense to him. He believes the Bible to be the inerrant word of God. Could it be that he's found a mistake?

Michael asks his pastor, who tells him to have faith. Usually Michael does have faith, but he's a bit older now and this time that answer isn't good enough. So he researches the apparent contradiction and discovers quite easily using the power of the internet that he was not the first person to realize this Biblical error. In fact, it is just one of hundreds more on a list.

Like Jason, Michael begins a quick descent down the slippery slope that leads to his eventual deconversion. But instead of anger, Michael experiences trauma. He is shell-shocked. Everything has been a lie and the carpet has been yanked out from underneath him.

Michael feels like reheated leftovers. He has never learned how to live life. He has almost no friends and doesn't know how to make more. He has no money and no skills to get a decent job because he assumed he would always work in the church. He suppressed his sexuality and doesn't know the first step to getting a girlfriend.

Michael wanders through the post-deconversion years like a lost spirit looking for a new body to inhabit—a body that has developed a life he can try on for size. He reaches out to other deconverted men who seem to be doing just fine. But when Michael hears their deconversion stories, he realizes they were not as "souled out" as he was. These other men built lives outside the Church while they were still in the fold. Back then, Michael would have considered them lukewarm. Now he considers them lucky.

Michael over-invested every part of himself into the Church and his religion. What was left, he prayed away. He desperately seeks a way to fill the void.

A Traumatized Empty Shell (TES) is defined as someone who has responded to their deconversion with a sense of crippling shock to the point where it is negatively impacting their lives. It's as if they've been zapped by a giant taser and the effects last for months or more.

This archetype is usually populated by former pastors, church workers, and missionaries whose entire life and livelihood was tied up in the church, but it can easily describe anyone who has spent in inordinate amount of time in religion.

The TES won't make meaningful strides to get better.

Rather, they respond to their deconversion by drifting snail-like through life. They live with a deep trepidation that prevents long-term happiness. To the people they meet, the TES comes off as empty, lethargic, and even boring.

Moving On

I have written about these two post-deconversion paths with a negative tone, but please understand that it is *normal* to pass through one of these phases. What isn't normal, and what I *am* concerned about, are men who spend way too long living as one of these archetypes.

The rest of this book is meant to help those who are ready to move on from one of these stages (or a stage that more uniquely describes your own story) and rebuild their lives.

I will offer mostly practical solutions, the ones I felt most benefited me when I went through my own transition. My desire has always been to *do*. I always have, and still crave, practical methods and concrete solutions to most any problem or negative circumstance. That was why the Perspectives class—which I mentioned in the previous chapter as having nearly saved my faith—resonated so strongly. It reframed the Christian lifestyle as something I could *do* rather than just *feel* during emotional praise songs.

Is it possible to have practical solutions in the wake of something so emotional and esoteric as deconversion from a religion? I think so.

Many people prefer abstract methods such as writing letters to their inner child or using essential oils. There is nothing wrong with these forms of therapy if you feel like they work for you. They have benefited, and still do benefit, thousands of deconverted people all over the planet. I probably would have come to terms with my own loss faster if I had tried them.

However, as men, our preference and inclination has always been to *do*. Thinking and feeling can only get us so far before we need to *take action*. Thus, practical solutions are what many men—like myself—seek when solving the problem of a traumatic deconversion.

Chapter 3

YOUR HAPPINESS

"The older I grow the more I distrust the familiar doctrine that age brings wisdom." — H.L. Mencken

I have said that the key to moving forward in a positive direction as a deconverted man is happiness. As a statement by itself, I realize that it's not very helpful. It could even be perceived as presumptuous.

Don't worry. I won't leave you hanging. We're going to dive deeply into this concept. You may even come to realize that years spent inside a fundamentalist religion have completely warped your idea of happiness, and that even to this day, you don't know what it truly means.

What the Church Teaches You about Happiness

In short, very little.

The Church doesn't address the topic of happiness because it doesn't consider it important. At worst, it considers the pursuit of personal happiness to be inappropriate or even sinful. Here are a few key maxims taught by the Church on happiness and why they're false.

Serve God and you will be happy.

This is so vague as to be meaningless. It encompasses a wide range of activities such as going to church, mission trips, praying, not sinning, and evangelizing. I suppose the church thinks that if you get all of that under control, you will finally be happy.

Serve others and you will be happy.

If you are brutally honest with yourself, you may admit that some acts of service simply don't gel with you and your personality. We can't admit this in our church circles because it makes us seem like bad Christians. Good Christians willingly help all people at all times, no matter what.

Here are some typical acts of service that I never really made peace with:

- **Donating time to nursing homes.** On several occasions, my youth group loaded us into the church van and dumped us at a nursing home with only a vague set of instructions, such as "Go show them love." Some kids excelled but I was totally lost in that environment.

- **Manual labor for the needy.** This is a popular

service-based mission trip that a lot of churches love. However, my penchant for logic and efficiency just couldn't reconcile with a strategy of assigning a bunch of untrained and inexperienced people to paint a house or build a fence.

- **Humanitarianism.** When a big storm hits a tropical island, I know how powerful the urge can be to rush in and help. In my opinion, the cost of feeding and sheltering you in the devastated location is too high when they should be feeding and sheltering their own population. It's better to hang back and let the affected community rebuild for themselves.

That's a tough list to look at. But the sooner we admit that we each have different abilities and ways of thinking, the sooner we can actually apply those strengths and make a real difference.

Pray and you will be happy.

Prayer often consists of sitting silently for a period of time and dwelling on all the non-optimal things in our lives and the lives of those we love, begging God to change those circumstances for the better. We are often met with silence or rejection of what we pray for.

I cannot fathom how prayer could *ever* make anyone feel happier. When we dwell on the negative, we perpetuate more negative.

Don't sin and you will be happy.

Remember that time you went to a party, drank too much, experimented with drugs, and hooked up with a girl? I bet you do because it was fun. The only thing that wasn't fun was the shame you felt the next day because you sensed God glaring down at you from heaven, hands on his hips.

Now that we know God doesn't exist, that feeling of shame should not exist either. All that remains is a hell of a memory that still makes you smile to this day.

Truth be told, most "sin" is fun, but much of what the Church considers sinful is associated with harsh lessons learned the hard way and better to avoid. But in so doing, you never really develop as a real human being or experience the richness of what life has to offer.

Surrender your life to Christ and you will be happy.

This effectively means giving up—throwing in the towel and saying, "I'm not even going to try."

Once a Christian surrenders his life to Christ, he can now safely sit in the passenger seat because Jesus has taken the wheel. Everything that transpires is simply God's intended plan. A man's life moves forward and happens *to* him without his active participation. He avoids taking responsibility and building his own life in accordance to his wishes.

Be thankful and you will be happy.

This fine bit of advice keeps you in suboptimal situations when you'd rather get out of them.

For example, let's say your job pays a good salary that supports you and your family, but it crushes your soul every day to go in. When you complain to your pastor, he will tell you that you should be thankful for what God has given you.

Be content and you will be happy.

This means you should settle for what you think God has given you. This kind of thinking keeps you from admitting that you want more out of life and are willing to go for it.

Fundamentalists Are Not Happy

Fundamentalists are one of the unhappiest groups of people on the planet. They'll tell you otherwise, but they are lying to themselves and to you.

It should be no surprise that fundamentalists are so unhappy because the very core of their doctrine is self-sacrifice at the expense of their own selves. Any attempt to achieve their own happiness is discouraged or considered sinful.

Instead, fundamentalists exert their efforts pursuing joy and make a distinction between happiness and joy. I definitely did. Maybe you did, too. What is that distinction?

Even when I was faithful, I couldn't quite grasp the concept of joy. Many a sermon expounded upon it and many Biblical passages address it. I knew I was supposed to experience it at all times, and when I didn't, I figured I was doing something wrong.

So, what is joy? First, we turn to Merriam-Webster:

1a: the emotion evoked by well-being, success, or good fortune or by the prospect of possessing what one desires.

1b: the expression or exhibition of such emotion.

2: a state of happiness or felicity.

Sounds pretty good to me. Many pastors will tell you that the Bible doesn't promise happiness but it does promise joy. That's weird, because according to the dictionary, happiness and joy seem to go hand in hand. Do fundamentalists think they don't? For that, we need to go back into the Bible. What does it have to say about joy? A lot, actually, so I'll only list a couple:

> *James 1:2-3: "Consider it pure joy, my brothers and sisters, whenever you face trials of many kinds, because you know that the testing of your faith produces perseverance."*

> *1 Peter 1:6-9: "In all this you greatly rejoice, though now for a little while you may have had to suffer grief in all kinds of trials. These have come so that the proven genuineness of your faith—of greater worth than gold, which perishes even though refined by fire—may result in praise, glory and honor when Jesus Christ is revealed. Though you have not seen him, you love him; an even though you do*

> *not see him now, you believe in him and are*
> *filled with an inexpressible and glorious joy,*
> *for you are receiving the end result of your*
> *faith, the salvation of your souls."*

It seems, according to the Bible, we should be experiencing joy even if bad stuff is happening. That's very different from the dictionary definition of joy.

I'm sure that, eventually, a Christian will read this and try to Greek me out of my point. But to us less intelligent folks stuck with our lowly English translations of the Bible, this is all we have to work with.

To me, if we take away all the Bible and church speak, joy in fundamentalism boils down to this: It's the positive emotion you're supposed to feel even when things are going wrong. Consider these examples:

- A thirteen-year-old girl gets cancer and dies. At her funeral, no one is happy but they are joyful because they know her death will be used by God for the greater good.

- A man's house burns down and he and his family lose everything they own. He isn't happy, but he maintains joy because he thinks God is using this situation to teach him something that will make him stronger.

- A man gets laid off from his job when his company downsizes. He has no idea where or when he'll get hired again and his late bills are piling up. He isn't happy, but he tries to force joy so he can see God's plan in the midst of his misfortune.

When I was a Christian, I would feel extreme guilt for not experiencing joy whenever I was going through challenging situations. Now, when I take a step back, it is abundantly clear why. I didn't experience joy because *it isn't normal to have positive emotions whenever really bad stuff is happening in your life.*

Duh!

This warped concept of joy is meant to anchor you in your fundamentalist beliefs whenever the all-powerful God allows devastating things to happen to you no matter what you feel or how your human logic interprets the situation. Fundamentalists discredit happiness and cling to joy, and assume that as long as they keep believing in God during bad situations, they will experience joy. Maybe. I certainly didn't.

If you think you are unhappy *because* you left your religion, that isn't the case. Now that you've left, you actually have the capacity to be far happier than the fundamentalists. You are no longer tied to the Biblical concept of joy but rather the Merriam-Webster version, which is defined as consistent happiness over a long period of time.

If you think it's unreasonable to live a life that is always "up-up-up-up" instead of "up-down-up-down," that's because you're still subconsciously buying into the Church concept that God puts you through trials and tribulations and that "up-up-up-up" is reserved only for heaven.

There *is* a way to design a consistently happy and joyful life. We'll explore that more in the next section.

The Aspect of Happiness that Everyone Forgets

In their efforts to be happy, most people pursue positive emotions and experiences. But almost everyone forgets to clear out the negative emotions and experiences—no matter how small—that clog up their daily lives. This pattern is subtly reinforced by the church because their definition of joy is designed to include the bad things that God purposely does to make you grow.

For example, let's say you love your church. Your pastor is witty, intelligent, and always teaches you something in his Sunday morning sermons. Listening to them makes you happy. Likewise, you love your men's Bible study group on Wednesday nights. The guys are great, everyone kicks back, and you learn edifying concepts that serve you in your daily life. Attending them makes you happy.

But you hate the job you go to every day of the week.

Your religion has promised that if you attend church and go to Bible study, you'll be happy (or joyful). God will bless you. But you have a nagging feeling in the back of your mind that you're not as happy as you could—or should—be.

Further, if you were to ask your pastor about the difficulties of your job, he'll probably tell you something about entrusting it to God or that God has you there for a reason. If you confide to your men's group that you're considering leaving your job because it doesn't make you happy (or fulfilled), they may remind you to consider God's plan (God's happiness) before your own, which basically means stuff your feelings, keep working, and be joyful anyway.

The Church teaches, or at least does not discourage, the idea that God puts us in unhappy situations for a reason, as part of a bigger plan. Further, we have to figure out how to be satisfied in that unhappy situation because God's plan is more important.

The fundamentalists who figure this out simply make their desired change and attribute the decision to God so that no one can argue with them. For example, after years at the same church, a pastor begins to have a different viewpoint on the Bible. The other pastors on staff don't agree with him. One month later, he finds a church in another city that is more in line with his new perspective and that will also pay him a higher salary. Suddenly, "God has spoken to him" and he moves. This is commonly dressed up as a "new season" in his life and ministry.

Where Does True Happiness Come From?

True, consistent, and long-term happiness is born from freedom.

Getting your salary transfer on payday will make you happy, but only until the next annoying thing happens. Spending the afternoon with your kids makes you happy, but only until one of your buddies pisses you off. Fitting in a good workout at the gym will make you happy, but only until your boss passes you up for a promotion.

Those temporary emotional spikes can make you happy, sure, but in order to experience long-term happiness, and given Merriam-Webster's definition of joy as something that endures over a sustained period of time, you need to be *free*.

People think of many different things when they hear

the word "freedom." This is because freedom is perceived differently depending on who you ask:

- One person might think he has all the freedom he needs simply because he lives in the United States of America.

- Another person may think he has all the freedom he needs because he has just been released from prison.

- Someone else may think he has all the freedom he needs because his boss has finally allowed him to work from home.

We need to go one step beyond defining freedom by what it means personally and reach for a more objective and practical definition. Why? Because when you define freedom only in terms of what it means to you, your brain tends to mold the word to your current situation which limits what it can really mean.

"Oh, freedom? Well, my house is paid off and I now have five weeks of vacation per year instead of two. So yeah, that's freedom to me."

Your brain then checks it off the mental list and moves on to the next thing. As men, our brains love nothing more than to consider a monumental matter "done and sorted" and permanently moved to the outbox.

There is nothing inherently wrong with that way of thinking, with being content with what we have. That's important. But sometimes I find that we forget to dream about something better because we are afraid that doing so belittles what we already have or makes it seem less important or presents a challenge we don't think we can meet.

This subtle line of thinking is a remnant from your fundamentalist days. The Church taught that you were supposed to be happy with where God had you in life and to not want more because the way things are were in accordance to his plan. Now that you know that God doesn't exist, you can explore what truly makes you free—and thus happier—without shame or guilt.

Fundamentalists Are not Free

"Freedom in Christ" is a misnomer because fundamentalists aren't free. There are countless rules and restrictions on their actions, thoughts, and feelings. But fundamentalists associate freedom with sin and so those restrictions serve a "higher purpose." But we all know a guy (or many) who has never stepped foot inside the local church and is a better person than many of the Christians within that church. That may have perplexed you when you were a fundamentalist, but it shouldn't anymore. You now know that freedom is not associated with "doing bad things."

Freedom is control. It means autonomy. It means taking responsibility for your life and steering yourself in the direction you want to go—regardless of what God or your pastors or your men's group wants.

Imagine you are free to do what you want, think what you want, feel what you want, go where you want, hang out with whoever you want, date whoever you want, buy whatever you want, accomplish whatever you want, and experience whatever you want without ever having to ask permission from anyone or pray for forgiveness. That is true freedom.

A man living this kind of life would be pretty darn happy. Countless men all over the world already live this way, and none of them belong to a fundamentalist religion.

At this point, you may start feeling some pushback. You may think I'm proposing an irresponsible, carefree life where nothing matters and we should indulge in all the fun, sinful behaviors we missed because now there are no consequences.

Not at all. Such a life would be chaos, and I can't stand chaos.

As I suggested before, removing your belief in God isn't enough. You may think it is, that it set you free, but are you really? There are a lot of practical areas in your life where the Church likely still has a strong influence. Seven in particular are most valuable to a man's life:

1. your money
2. your health
3. your family
4. your social life
5. your hobbies
6. your relationships with women
7. your spirituality

The Church has taught you a lot of wrong information about these seven life areas and, as a result, you may still carry some negative beliefs about them even after you've left the faith. These falsehoods need to be cleared out.

The next chapter will expand on these seven life areas.

Then, in the second section of the book, we will dive deeply into each one. I will show you what the Church teaches about each life area, explain why it's wrong, and give you practical steps for how to re-align that part of your life in the right direction as a newly deconverted man.

Chapter 4

THE SEVEN LIFE AREAS

"Happiness is not a matter of intensity but of balance, order, rhythm and harmony." — Thomas Merton

In the previous chapter, I listed the seven life areas that have the most practical and immediate effects on your overall happiness. In this chapter, I will demonstrate why.

Remember: Happiness is a two-tiered concept. It requires the presence of positive emotions and experiences *and* the absence of negative emotions and experiences. To get us started, imagine the following scenarios:

Your Money

Positive

Do you remember your first real paycheck and what it

meant? Financial security, a safety net. Now you could buy that expensive thing you wanted or move out of your parent's house. Maybe you could finally take the vacation you'd always dreamed of. You were free from having to rely on someone else to pay your expenses for you.

Negative

Imagine you've been laid off from your job. The economy is bad and no one in your field is hiring. To make ends meet, you have to grind sixty hours a week at some random job that doesn't pay what you're worth. The rent is late. You've accumulated credit card debt with rapidly rising interest costs. It feels like you'll need a miracle to get out from under the debt.

Your Health

Positive

After years of inactivity, junk food, and drinking, you decide to set a goal to run a marathon. You cut out all trashy food and eat well. You train consistently over time. The fat melts off, revealing a body you haven't seen since high school. You feel the effects of the training spilling into other areas of your life. You have more energy for your job, your mind is sharp, and you feel cleaner from the healthy diet. The marathon arrives and you finish it.

Negative

You live off fast food and soft drinks. You were naturally skinny when you were younger, but now you're older and your metabolism has slowed. Your belly expands and begins to hang. You're always fatigued and lethargic so you drink high-sugar energy drinks to keep up at work. Your increased weight strains your joints and back. Your doctor prescribes medicine and tells you to avoid strenuous exercise. Your medicine causes side effects, which require more medicine to fix. This downward spiral continues indefinitely.

Your Family

Positive

You grew up in a family where both your parents supported your ideas, dreams, and goals. They encouraged you no matter what, even if you chose to take a different approach to life than they did—including your spiritual or religious choices or lack thereof.

Negative

You had overbearing parents who were too protective when you were young and didn't allow you to grow and develop at your own pace. Instead of supporting you in your choices, they were often disappointed that you didn't show interest in what they thought was best for you: sports, going to medical school, becoming a pastor, or taking over the family business.

Your Social Life

Positive

You have a wide network of solid, positive, and funny men with whom you are in regular contact. The group text message chat is always pinging with funny memes and college football predictions. You get together once a week for dinner or beers. Once a year, you travel together. If you need help moving something, your buddy is there with his truck, no questions asked, because you did the same for him a few weekends ago. If you need relationship advice, these guys have you covered because they've been there, done that.

Negative

You graduated college but didn't make an effort to keep up with your guy friends. It's Friday night but no one's calling or messaging. When you reach out, they either don't respond or say they're "too busy." You note that they don't invite you to wherever they're going that night. You know Brad and Tyler from the office, but the only thing you have in common with them is that you happen to work the same job.

Your Hobbies

Positive

You join a flag football team that has games every Saturday. After a long week of working in a cramped cubicle at the office, it feels great to get outside with a fun group of guys and play a casual, competitive game.

Negative

You work a job that requires you to always be available. Your cell phone never stops ringing and every email is marked with the urgent red "!" symbol. Your guitar sits in the corner collecting dust and you keep skipping weekend camping trips with your buddies. You've convinced yourself that you'll have time for your hobbies "someday," but the projects at work just keep piling up.

Your Relationships with Women

Positive

Remember the first time you kissed a girl? Or the first time you had sex? You likely felt exhilarated, validated, and accepted as if you'd finally been allowed into an exclusive club of men. Everything felt right. Your relationship life had officially begun.

Negative

Perhaps you once asked a girl out but she wasn't interested in you "like that." Maybe she told you that she felt you were more like a friend or a brother. You stick around, hoping she eventually changes her mind, but she doesn't. Still, your feelings for her grow. She starts dating someone else, someone you think isn't good for her. Your heart feels a heavy, dull ache every day.

Your Spirituality

Positive

Remember that time you went to church camp or a retreat and the gospel made sense to you for the first time? In a highly emotional state, you surrendered your life to Jesus, and in that instant, everything aligned and you finally had a purpose. You felt loved and accepted by both God—the creator of the universe—and the Christian community.

Negative

After many years—perhaps your entire life—in the Church, you have questions about your faith. You ask your friends and pastors but their responses aren't satisfying. In secret, you look to other sources. You find a breadth of information revealing, all at once and harshly, that the faith you've been dedicated to doesn't actually make any sense. You feel hurt and betrayed. Your church casts you out. In one fell swoop, you've lost your community, friends, and purpose in life.

Rank Yourself

It's unlikely that your entire life is a dumpster fire. You are probably doing fine in some areas and not so great in others. This is why you experience some "meh" days. If you've ever experienced a truly bad day, it's probably because one or more of the negative life areas above took over and you didn't get a chance to experience the positive ones.

Now go back and rank each of those life areas on a scale from 1 to 10, with 1 being "horrific nightmare" and 10 being "absolute perfection." If you have a physical copy of this book, write the number next to the heading. If you have the digital version, write your rankings down in the notebook you used to use for taking notes during sermons or Bible studies.

There are no right or wrong answers. Jesus isn't looking over your shoulder. The most important thing is to be *completely honest* with yourself. These rankings will help you later in Part 3 of this book as you make a plan to reshape your life moving forward.

Balance Matters

Unhappiness, or a feeling that "something is missing," comes when one or more of the seven life areas are out of balance. Consider the following examples:

- The man who hits the gym every day with jacked biceps, round pecs, and awesome abs but has very little money. He doesn't have time to make more because he's always at the gym.

- The man who hangs out with guy friends four nights a week. They drink beer, eat chicken wings, watch sports, and share hilarious stories and inside jokes. But all that unhealthy food and beer go straight to his gut and he gets winded walking up his apartment steps.

- The man with a thriving business that churns $50,000 profit per month. He's financially secure and can buy all the toys he wants but his wife doesn't respect him—or even like him—and always picks fights with him when he comes home from work.

- The man who has over-dedicated himself to his spiritual practice: crippling minimalism, days-long meditation retreats, vows of silence and excessive fasting. But he has no money, friends, girlfriends, or hobbies. Ouch.

Fundamentalist pastors across the globe regularly declare that good things such as adequate finances, healthy relationships, or plenty of friends don't bring true happiness and that true happiness can only be found in Jesus. Pastors (and others) who say this are out of balance because they have life areas that are lacking. They mistakenly believe that Jesus fills the gaps in their happiness rather than achieving a more holistic balance between their life areas.

In reality, if anyone were to just raise the quality of the life areas that are falling behind instead of trying to polish themselves with Jesus, then they'll quickly realize that Jesus and God aren't really necessary for true happiness.

How We Get Out of Balance

Men tend to deeply pursue accomplishment in one specific area, usually one we are already naturally good at. That's because we are creatures of action. When we experience achievement, we get addicted to the feeling and dedicate even more time to perpetuating that experience. We love feeling like experts. We all want to be the go-to guy for something.

As a result, other areas of our lives suffer. Even when we become aware of the pattern, we usually shrug and say, "Well, I'm just not very good at x, but I'm awesome at y." Over time, our seven life areas become more imbalanced, which means we won't be as happy (or free) as we could be.

The Church and the Seven Life Areas

The Church positions itself as an authority over the seven life areas and instructs us in the godly way to engage in them, which I came to realize are usually completely wrong. To me, this is far more insidious than the supernatural religious dogma it teaches. When the Church sinks its teeth into the practical and real-world areas of our lives, it is much harder to uproot its influences.

These are the lasting effects we carry even after leaving fundamentalism—the practical cracks we need to clean out if we are ever to be truly free. It's why I wrote earlier that simply ceasing to believe in the existence of God is not enough.

When the Church steps in and tells us how to structure the seven life areas in accordance to its teachings, we end up with a less-than-optimal life. Men who are naturally good at certain things will tragically discard these aspects of themselves—these strengths—because the Church made them feel it was the right thing to do. Consider the following examples:

- The naturally gifted salesman who donates all his high earnings to a megachurch because he thinks rich people struggle to inherit the kingdom of God.
- The naturally gifted would-be father who forgoes a family because Paul said it's better for his ministry to be single.
- The naturally gifted athlete who skips the NFL draft because he thinks fame and fortune are sinful.

These sacrifices are then highly praised by the Church, which congratulates that man for laying his gifts at the feet of the Lord. This positive reinforcement leads this man to think he's done the right thing, perhaps never realizing that he's allowed the Church to detrimentally influence his future. Then, later in life, when he feels that God that hasn't given him the happiness he secretly feels he deserves because of his sacrifice and obedience, he wonders what went wrong.

Some Tips for Part 2 of this Book

This book is about practicality. It's about getting your life back in the way that *you* want and with a balance that works *for you*. To that end, each chapter in the next section is dedicated to one of the seven life areas identified above. They can be read in any order, but I strongly recommend that you eventually read them all, ideally more than once.

Also, don't try to address all seven areas at once—doing so will overwhelm you and spread you too thin; you won't make meaningful progress quickly. Choose two life areas and focus on building them up first. And don't immediately choose the chapter on relationships with women. I know you guys. You'll probably want to skip right to that, thinking it's the juiciest bit, but please resist. There's a reason why I placed it next to last.

Did you rank the seven with a number from 1 through 10 as I suggested earlier? Use those rankings to help you decide which ones you'll address first. I recommend tackling your lowest-ranked areas sooner rather than later because they are likely contributing the most to your current unhappiness.

For me, it was Money and Health, and the same has been true for many other men. Read those chapters to learn why I recommend them first for all recently-deconverted men looking to build a new life and identity outside the sphere of organized religion. But don't force it; they may not be appropriate. We all have different needs. Be true to yours.

Act and Implement

I can't repeat this enough: You must *act* and *implement*. The information in this book only represents *potential* energy. It won't help you unless you harness and actualize it into your own life.

You are a man, and therefore that means you are a creature of action. You like to do. You feel physically uncomfortable when you know that something important is left undone. These masculine traits inherent within you will serve you well as you rebuild your life.

As you read further, a lot of you will probably think to yourself, "Wow, this isn't easy."

You would be correct.

If you think about it, there is nothing easier than a fundamentalist life lived in a fundamentalist community within the walls of the Church. You were told that if you relinquished all desires and responsibility to God, he would take care of you completely. Then you'd get to spend an eternity in heaven where everything is great, without hardships or challenges.

Of all the people on earth, fundamentalists are some of the most guilty of "coasting" through life because they've always been taught that life on earth is less important than the one to come after "God brings you home."

Now that we are free and clear of *that* fantasy, the time for easy living is over. I'm calling you to something higher and better. Building it will take work, discipline, and time, but I am confident that as you read on, you will see the merits of the kind of life I prescribe in this book. It's a life of freedom, happiness, abundance, and independence where you live by your own standards—not the ones assigned by your 60-year-old pastor or a 2,000-year-old book.

PART II

Chapter 5
YOUR MONEY

"If we command our wealth, we shall be rich and free; if our wealth commands us, we are poor indeed." —Edmund Burke

I grew up with frugal parents. We were never rich, but I don't remember my family ever having money problems. This is because both my mom and dad were careful with their money and this rubbed off on me.

When I was about nine or ten, I started getting a small allowance. Over time, I've noticed that when kids come to possess any amount of money, what they do next—whether they spend it immediately or save it—will often predict how they will treat their money in the future. Because of the mindset I picked up from my parents, I saved mine and kept it in my bottom drawer in a Power Rangers wallet. Whenever I wanted to buy something, I would reluctantly dip in, but I would also carefully count what remained.

My dad would often forget to give me my allowance. When I asked, he just shrugged.

I don't believe this was a calculated lesson, but it did teach me a valuable truth: My source of income—my allowance—was unreliable, which pushed me to save even more.

Around that time, I went to a friend's house and got my first taste of the Nintendo 64 gaming console. If you're my age, you remember exactly how it felt to pick up one of those magical, triple-pronged controllers for the first time and play those groundbreaking games in a mind-blowing 3D environment.

I had to have one.

Using toy magazines, I wrote down the price of the console, the controllers, and the games that I wanted. I added up the total and immediately rushed to my bottom drawer and forced the Red Ranger to cough up the dough. I counted. I didn't have enough. I wasn't even close.

All my careful saving *still* didn't allow me to buy what I wanted. This is my earliest memory of experiencing the cruel taste of not being able to afford something I desperately desired. I resolved to increase my saving further. This frugality stayed with me as I grew older.

As I approached high school graduation, the big question loomed over my head: What did I want to do with my life?

Like a good, obedient fundamentalist, I turned to God for an answer. I had always been taught that whatever career I eventually chose, whatever lifestyle I had, and however much money I ultimately earned were all predetermined by God in accordance to his plan.

All I had to do was divine God's plan amidst prayer and "being faithful."

When I was a college student, I worked full-time

summer jobs that paid pretty well but I would save all that money and frugally use it to survive the school year so I could focus on my studies without working. But I still dutifully tithed on my meager income.

I had faith that what the pastor said was true: My tithes were especially valuable because I didn't have a lot and that God would eventually bless me because of my giving. The pastor always appended that with a quick "not necessarily financially" when he preached about said blessings, but I kept my fingers crossed for the cash anyway.

I also believed that it was better to *not* have a lot of money. After all, the Bible said it was difficult for a rich man to enter the kingdom of heaven, and I definitely didn't need any more temptations than the ones I was already struggling with.

After I graduated college, I got my first "real job" and two weeks later, my first "real paycheck." It had more digits than any check I'd ever seen in my life. I was on top of the world. I allowed myself to momentarily forget about being frugal and bought myself a mountain bike. After that, though, I was back to saving.

I didn't change my lifestyle with my new income. Frugality had been ingrained too deeply in me to do that. So, for the first time in my life, I was able to start saving significant money. I didn't know what it would all be for, but I saved regardless. To me, God had really come through. I had prayed faithfully to seek out his plan, followed it, and now I was being rewarded.

A couple of years later, I had the sudden realization that my current lifestyle wouldn't last forever. I was a childless single guy renting a house with his college buddies who never traveled. It was a lifestyle I could afford, but it was time for a change.

I let it go and left it up to God. He had brought me this far and he wouldn't abandon me. When the time came to "enter a new season," I had faith that God would bring the appropriate extra income into my life. For that reason, I never seriously crunched the numbers.

A few years later, after I deconverted, I turned my attention back to my job and my financials. I finally admitted that no plan of God had brought me to my current circumstances, which were now less than ideal for that new stage of my life—that was all on me.

I further admitted that all the money I needed or *wanted* to earn would also be up to me. I realized that if I was going to develop my life beyond bare-bones frugality and into one that I was enthusiastic about, I was going to need more money.

It was finally time to sort my financial structures in accordance to *my plan*, not God's.

What the Church Teaches You About Money

When I was young, much of what I learned about money came from watching my parents. But when I was older, what I learned about money came from the church. And even years after deconverting, those teachings were still rooted in my subconscious—that money is a source of temptation, that rich people are evil, and that desiring more money made me selfish or greedy. There's a high probability that you also still harbor these false beliefs.

Now, on the other side of fundamentalism, I've been

able to rearrange and redefine my relationship with money, and my hope is to help you do the same.

The Bible teaches quite a lot about money, much of which is *true*. The writers of the Bible commend hard work that leads to financial prosperity and recommend this way of life. Most of these verses are found in the Book of Proverbs.

> *Proverbs 10:4: "Lazy hands make for poverty, but diligent hands bring wealth."*
>
> *Proverbs 14:23: "All hard work brings a profit, but mere talk leads only to poverty."*
>
> *Proverbs 13:16: "All who are prudent act with knowledge, but fools expose their folly."*
>
> *Proverbs 27: 23-24: "Be sure you know the condition of your flocks, give careful attention to your herds; for riches do not endure forever, and a crown is not secure for all generations."*
>
> *Proverbs 21:20: "The wise store up choice food and olive oil, but fools gulp theirs down."*

These verses are wise and timeless. They instruct you to work diligently, know the state of your financial affairs and assets, invest and save your earnings for the future, and not be lazy. I cannot argue against any of these verses. When the Bible isn't talking about God, there are a lot of gems to be found.

But what about the Church? In general, the Church, Church culture, and fundamentalism are quite negative toward money. Some of the Church's favorite verses—mostly found in the New Testament—are presented in conjunction with God and Jesus. They are cherry-picked by pastors because they provide good fuel for guilt-inducing sermons that chastise congregations across the globe about their materialism. Here are some popular ones that you probably know:

> *1 Timothy 6:10: "For the love of money is a root of all kinds of evil. Some people, eager for money, have wandered from the faith and pierced themselves with many griefs."*
>
> *Matthew 6:19-21: "Do not store up for yourselves treasures on earth, where moths and vermin destroy, and where thieves break in and steal. But store up for yourselves treasures in heaven, where moths and vermin do not destroy, and where thieves do not break in and steal. For where your treasure is, there your heart will be also."*
>
> *Proverbs 11:28: "Those who trust in their riches will fall, but the righteous will thrive like a green leaf."*
>
> *Proverbs 11:4: "Wealth is worthless in the day of wrath, but righteousness delivers from death."*

Also Matthew 6:24-34. This one is long so I won't

write it out here, but this is Jesus's well-known, "No man can serve two masters" discourse.

Those last two Proverbs verses are especially interesting because the writer changes his tune when he brings God, Jesus, and "the end times" into the conversation.

So you see that while the Bible has a combination of money truths and money falsehoods, the modern Church tends to take the route of shaming the rich and the desire for money.

Fundamentalist religion appeals to the state of being poor because Jesus, the disciples, Paul, and a host of other Bible characters were also poor. The writers of the Bible play this up as a virtue, stating that their poverty allowed them to focus better on God. The point is further made when wealthy Bible figures, such as Solomon, insist that wealth is meaningless (Ecclesiastes).

Fundamentalists tend to use these stories as excuses to ignore their financial lives. The implication of pursuing money would be that they inherently don't trust God to take care of them. Wanting more money was greedy. It meant you weren't living right and should adjust your lifestyle. Seeking more money meant you needed to examine your heart. If you found yourself in a low-paying job, well, God put you there for a reason that he will reveal in his own time (or never).

The Church considers all money as belonging to God and that you are only a temporary steward of that money (never mind that you spent forty hours of your life at a desk that week in exchange for it). In this way, the Church placed itself as an authority over your money and strongly influenced what you did with it, making sure you spent it in ways that "glorified God."

A common complaint of my generation (for context, I was born in 1988) is that our schools never taught us about financial literacy, saving, or investing. As a result, much of what we think and feel about money was indoctrinated into us by the Church. Clearing out the Church's incorrect view of money is, in my opinion, one of the most overlooked aspects of recovering from fundamentalism, and one of the most important.

If you can get this area right, you can massively change your life for the better.

Yes, Money Does Buy Happiness

Everyone's familiar with the phrase, "Money doesn't buy happiness." It isn't true.

- If you have loads of credit card debt, you are less happy than you could be.
- If you are debt free but don't have enough money left over for retirement, then you are less happy than you could be.
- If you are debt free and are actively saving for retirement but don't have enough money left over to send your kid to college, then you are less happy than you could be.

This thought exercise could go on forever. Those who claim that money doesn't buy happiness would point to this same example to prove their own point. That is, no matter how much money you have, you will always find something else to want and therefore you will never be as happy as you could be. Such people have an incorrect view of what money really is. They think it is merely a medium of exchange in which you buy your wants and satisfy your needs, but that is far too simplistic.

Money is a tool, and tools can be leveraged. It's true that if you use your limited tools (your money) to buy impulse consumer products and gadgets, you likely won't find lasting happiness. In the example above, I didn't talk about the latest smart phone or sixty-inch televisions. But if you leverage your tools to take advantage of money's most powerful—and often overlooked—attributes, then you will be *much* happier, and that happiness will last.

What are the attributes of money that will make you happy? I'm glad you asked.

Money Is Security

Despite God promising to prosper you and not to harm you (Jeremiah 29:11), bad stuff still happens to believers and non-believers alike. These problems can often be solved with money.

Most people live paycheck to paycheck. If you aren't financially secure, you aren't secure in the true meaning of the word. If you aren't secure, you will live in a constant state of stress worrying about the next big financial setback. Stress is the enemy of happiness.

Security takes many different forms:

Big Household Expenses

Eventually, your refrigerator *will* go out and need to be replaced. Your air conditioner *will* break, probably right at the beginning of summer. A big storm *will* come at some point and drop a large branch onto your roof.

If you have the money to deal with such adversities when they come up (and they will), you won't be nearly as stressed as your neighbor who is not as prepared.

Medical Care

If you are an American or live in a country that doesn't have socialized medicine, you will foot most or all of the medical bills that your insurance doesn't cover. Are you one emergency room visit away from a financial tailspin?

Retirement

Investments can ensure that money will be available in the future when you don't want to (or can't) work anymore.

Protection

You may think your police force or government are there to protect you and your family, but this is incorrect. These two entities offer justice, not protection.

The police can't stop someone from breaking into your house or car. They can find and arrest the thief afterward, but at that point you've already lost your possessions. They can't stop someone from murdering you. They can find and arrest the murderer afterward, but at that point you're already dead.

True protection comes from money. If you have more money, you can afford to live in a safer neighborhood.

You can afford an advanced security system. You can afford to take safer means of transportation.

There is a reason celebrities, politicians, and wealthy businessmen use some of their money to hire private security and bodyguards—because they know the police can't protect them from people who really want to hurt them. And for that, you have to pay.

Extreme Circumstances

If you have money, you can leave your city or country in the event of a civil war, attacks from abroad, or natural catastrophes. These things are unlikely, of course, but it's always good to have a Plan B or even C, and those will require some extra cash.

Money Is Time

Although people usually quote the reverse, money allows you to buy back your time. This is quite possibly the most valuable use of your money. Why? Because time is your only nonrenewable resource. You can always make more money, but you can never make more time.

- If you have enough money, you can pay for a house cleaning service rather than spending a weekend afternoon doing it yourself.
- If you have enough money, you can take the faster train instead of the cheaper, slower bus.
- If you have enough money, you can splurge for that direct flight and eliminate the four-hour stopover.

Fundamentalists really miss the mark on this concept because they don't value time. They consider time to be infinite because of the eternity they think they'll spend in heaven.

If these thoughts still linger in your brain from years spent in the Church, you need to clear them out as fast as possible. Sit down and dwell on the importance of time and how dangerous it is to waste it. This life is all we get, and while there is plenty of time for exciting and interesting distractions, none of that time should be squandered. Having more money can give you more options on how to buy back your time and life.

Money Is Freedom

It is possible to eventually have more money than you can feasibly spend during the remainder of your life. If you accumulate such an amount, you can quit your day job and buy back forty hours per week, every week! You can invest it strategically to generate enough monthly interest to live off the income without ever working again. This is perhaps money's greatest attribute: It can be leveraged to free you of the need to invest more of your time into earning more money.

This is called financial freedom. To most of you reading this, financial freedom is a far-off concept reserved only for those elderly, retired folks who have "earned" their right (and enough money) to stop working. But you know as well as I that the idea and comfort of traditional retirement is dwindling in the modern era. Our employers pay too little, stuff costs too much, and interest rates on our savings are in the gutter.

Retirement isn't dead yet although it needs to be redefined for our times. If you have a rough idea of how much money you'll need for the rest of your life, it is possible to work toward that goal and achieve it. Best of all, you probably don't have to wait until you're 65.

The key to achieving this freedom is to understand the difference between spending and investing, and disciplining yourself to do more investing than spending.

When you *spend* your money, it's gone forever. This happens when you buy electronics, Netflix subscriptions, and new cars. When you *invest* your money, you purchase something that will eventually bring money back to you in the future. This happens when you buy rental real estate, index funds, retirement accounts, or a wide range of other investment options.

This is an overly simplified explanation of how increasing your investments and decreasing your spending and expenses can lead to financial freedom. For now, it will serve you to create an itemized budget of where your money goes each month and then start making adjustments for bettering your financial future.

How Money Enters Your Life

I'm sure you're familiar with the formula: You go to your job every weekday and money is direct-deposited into your account either biweekly or monthly. Through the fundamentalist lens, God gave you that job and so therefore God provided you with the money.

But let's break this down with reality in mind. You don't get paid just for showing up to work with a smile on your face and a spring in your step and a prayer in your heart. You get paid because of the *value* you offer your employer.

Let's say you're an accountant. Your employer, who owns the company, needs an accountant because has no idea how to keep the books himself. So he pays you for your knowledge and skills. The moment you stop doing that (stop providing *value*), your boss stops paying you, fires you, and hires the next accountant. That's simply how business works. Your boss doesn't just pray to God to give him a solution to his accounting needs.

People who provide value get paid for that value. The more value you offer, the more money you are paid.

Value is certainly relative and not always what we think it should be. This explains why, for example, NFL players get paid much more than medical doctors. A doctor provides his value to one patient at a time throughout the day. An NFL player provides value to the tens of thousands of fans who show up to the game, as well as the millions of people who tune in on television. Thus, the NFL player is paid more despite the less noble nature of his work compared to the doctor. Also, because the NFL is a multi-billion dollar industry, there is simply a bigger pot of money to play with.

Here's another example. Imagine two pastors. One works at a megachurch and the other at a small Baptist church on the corner. The megachurch's average Sunday attendance is 15,000 while the small Baptist church attracts about 45. These two pastors preach the same gospel, same beliefs, and same message. They both take up an offering after the sermon.

Who makes more money? The megachurch pastor because he provides value to more people.

The church oftentimes demonizes rich people as "greedy" or "selfish," but how did they become rich in the first place? Unless they stole their money, most of them provided value to a large number of people:

- Anyone who creates a small computer that fits in your pocket and sells it to millions of people is going to become rich.
- Anyone who creates a revolutionary social media website used by billions of people is going to become rich.
- Anyone who creates an online retail store that drop-ships whatever people want on their doorsteps anywhere in the entire world is going to become rich.

I point this out because there's a high chance you still have Church clutter in your head about money being bad or rich people being greedy or evil. These thoughts can prevent you from inviting more money into your own life.

When you pursue more money, you aren't being greedy or selfish. You are seeking resources for your security, time, and freedom while simultaneously providing honest value to people. It's a win-win.

So now that you understand why and how money comes into your life, that it isn't evil, that you receive it for providing value to people, and that more is better, how do you go about getting more of it? If you guessed, "Provide more value to more people," you are correct. I will discuss strategies for doing this later in this chapter. But first, I need to make something clear.

Frugality Isn't Always the Answer

By now, I hope you are gaining a new perspective about money and are already thinking of ways to repurpose your cash to contribute to your security, time, and freedom. Perhaps you are making a mental list of all the things you need to cut out—Starbucks coffee, sports channels, the motorcycle in the garage—to save money and accomplish these goals. It's all gotta go!

Don't do it.

There is nothing inherently wrong with this, but is it the *best* way? Is living frugally like the Church and Dave Ramsey told us to do the best solution? That insistent pressure to not "store up our treasure on earth" was very real. Frugality was celebrated and praised because it was how Jesus lived.

As I stated earlier in this book, I believe that *happiness* should be our primary goal. Unless you're a committed minimalist (I'm not), cutting out the minor pleasures in your life will have little impact on financial security but it will likely make you less happy. Frugality does have its merits, but there's a limit beyond which we start to make ourselves miserable. And now that you've broken free of the guilt for wanting more money, you no longer need to resort to extreme frugality to fix your money problems. You can finally consider the alternative:

Make more money.

Making more money will bring you security *and* allow you to buy back your time *and* become financially free. This will increase your happiness by leaps and bounds.

I know. Easier said than done. Making more money is a challenge, but just like working out, it will be worth the effort. Those extra zeroes in your bank account will leave a big fat grin on your face.

The ideas I list below will take some time for most people to implement—including me—but that does not mean they are not worth doing. Any work that improves the quality of your life and happiness is *always* worth doing, no matter how long it takes.

So, let's start to answer the million-dollar question (literally) that most people on the planet have asked themselves at some point in their lives: How can I make more money?

Money-Making Strategies

That's a seductive heading, but the goal is very practical: finding ways to use your career to generate more income and financial security.

Find a New Job (and Do It Often)

If you're not enjoying a relationship, you break up and meet someone else. Likewise, if you feel you don't make enough money from your job to live the kind of lifestyle you want live, find one that pays you better.

The days of our fathers are over. They worked at one job their entire lives, retired, then lived off their fat pensions and company perks. They were able to stay at these jobs their entire careers because, back then, employers regularly gave reasonable promotions and raises.

These days, that ain't happening.

Therefore, you should have no qualms about checking

relevant job postings at least once a month and monkey-branching to one of your company's competitors if they offer a better salary. If an interviewer asks why you only stay at jobs for two years, tell him or her you've been looking for more challenging work and your previous position wasn't offering the development and learning opportunities you wanted.

Reduce Your Work Hours

Parkinson's Law states that "work expands to fill the time available for its completion."

If you work a standard eight-hour office job, you've probably noticed that you only spend about four of those hours—and that's being generous—*actually* working. The rest of the time is spent having coffee, chatting with your coworkers, and messing around on your computer or cell phone.

If you discipline yourself and make it clear to your coworkers that you are not to be disturbed in the morning, you can likely finish your day's work before lunch. If there are simply too many office distractions, talk to your boss and see if you can negotiate some "work from home" days. Since your job is probably computer-based anyway, see if he or she will let you work remotely and only come in for important meetings. If yes, you can still knock out a day's work in the first four hours of your morning. But it will take some discipline.

If you can reduce the amount of time you spend at the office, then you will have given yourself an automatic raise because you've essentially increased your per-hour income. Even if you're salaried, you can still figure out your hourly rate. And then you can decide what to do with all that extra time. Maybe find a part-time job or pursue a professional dream and make some more money? More on this below.

Geoarbitrage

This is a fancy word for working abroad.

Many countries offer tax-free income, higher salaries, and good benefits packages for foreign workers. They do this to attract the skills and expertise that are lacking in their own country. Just reducing—or even eliminating—your taxes by not working and residing inside your home country will be enough to dramatically increase your income.

I lived and worked in the Middle East for a couple of years and have many positive things to say about the experience—the money I earned being one of them.

If finding a new job, reducing your work hours, or going overseas don't vibe with you or apply to the work you do, then consider building more income sources. This is my preferred way to increase my income.

How to Build Income Sources

You may think that your job is the only source of income you will ever have or *should* have. This could be leftover subconscious programming from your Church days that had you believing that God placed you in that job for reasons known only to him.

Now that you know this isn't the case, you can reframe your job as what it really is—an *income source*.

And there is no rule or law that says you can only have one income source. Not even your boss can prevent you from having other means of making money.

An income source can be anything as long as money flows from it into your bank account. It could be rent checks from real estate you own or an investment account that earns interest. It could be a rare coin collection you sell or money generated from a pyramid scheme you're running (but hopefully not!). You could even "start a business," though for many the idea brings up mental images of a building with inventory and employees that costs tens of thousands of dollars to run with lots of paperwork. But that is no longer true. There are many low-cost models depending on what you are trying to sell —buyers are a click away.

People who have a lot of money almost always have multiple sources of income. If you want to make more money, then your goal should be to increase the number of *sources* of income you have flowing into your life.

On the flip side are "side hustles," a term that has been floating around the internet for a while. In fact, it has become so overused that most people roll their eyes when they hear it. Not only that, it enforces the idea that what you're doing is only "on the side"—even if it's super valuable to a lot of people and customers—and that it doesn't deserve a significant amount of your time and attention.

Side hustles are usually associated with activities in which you directly exchange time for money, such as driving for Uber or being a personal trainer on the weekends. Those services are great for some quick cash, but ideally you'll want to build something that's more sustainable.

These many options are why I prefer the term "income source." Anything can be an income source if it brings money into your life. If you can create and deliver value to people, you will make money. And delivering value basically means that you can fix someone's problem.

So how do you get started doing that?

Step 1: Determine what skill, knowledge, expertise, or experience you have to offer.

Remember, money is made by bringing value to people who then pay you for it. To make money, you essentially need to solve problems for people.

All products and services that exist today came about as a way to solve a problem.

- People didn't like getting wet in the rain so someone invented the umbrella.
- People didn't like using the bathroom outside so someone invented the toilet.
- People didn't like, or didn't know how, to build their own houses, so someone started a construction company.

Some problems have even been solved more than once: Telegrams turned into landlines which then turned into cell phones. Cassette tapes turned into CDs which then turned into mp3s. Hell, new models of computers that improve upon the previous version are released every year.

Make a list of all the skills, knowledge, expertise, and experiences you've accumulated over your life that you can offer to others. What do you know and what are you good at?

I realize this can be surprisingly difficult. A long time spent in the Church has taught us that pride is bad, that all good things about us are really gifts from God, that we should submit all our successes to God, and loads of other false teachings that make it challenging for us to accurately self-assess what we're good at.

A great place to start is what you do for your day job. You have that job because your employer is willing to pay you for the value you bring and the problem you solve for him. As I said earlier, there is no rule or law that says your job has to be your only income source. You can take that very same knowledge or skill and build another income source with it, whether that be on a freelance basis or an entire business that you own and control.

Another great way of uncovering what you are good at is to simply ask your friends, family, or other people who know you well. They often have a different perspective of you than you have of yourself. When you ask them, listen out for things like

- "Are you serious? You're a pro at ____!"
- "Every time I need ____ you're the guy I go to."
- "You're the best person I know at ____."

Whatever they fill in the blank with is a strong indication of the value you can bring. Here are a few examples to get you started thinking about what you have that can be used to bring value to people and monetized:

- Public speaking

- Web design
- Writing and/or editing
- Organizing data and spreadsheets
- Cooking
- Mechanical skills
- Hospitality experience
- Filmmaking
- Audio production/editing
- Travel expertise

Step 2: Identify a group of people that you can bring value to.

Now that you know what skill or knowledge you have that brings value, you need to decide precisely *who* you will bring that value to.

To get some ideas, practice viewing the world as consisting of groups of people whose problems you can practically solve with the skill or knowledge that you identified in the previous step. These groups are also known as your "target market." Ideally this should be a group of people you already know a lot about or could learn about reasonably quickly. Some examples include:

- health care professionals
- gym owners
- parents of young children
- elderly people

No product or service sells everything to everyone, so you need to decide what you can offer and then who needs it most. The more precisely you can define a market and its needs, the better. This is called a "market niche."

- Health care professionals who are approaching retirement and want to work abroad as their final job.
- Gym owners who want to branch out their personal training services into the online space.
- Parents of young children who want a program to teach their children a new language.
- Elderly people who live alone and want to learn how to use their new iPhones to keep in touch with their friends.

I know it seems counterintuitive to purposely reduce the potential pool of people you can sell to, but that's how it works. When people in your target niche market find the precise, perfect product or service that solves their specific need, they will

- gladly pay for it without having to be sold on it.
- pay more because they haven't found their specific solution anywhere else.
- repeatedly buy from you for the same reason as above.

For example, if you're an accountant and you start offering services on a freelance basis, it will be hard to compete with the other big accounting firms in your city. But if you offer accounting services *only* for private physical therapy clinics (as just one of many possibilities), then those clinics will be more likely to work with you than those big, general firms because your clients know you will give them expert service based on the specific needs of running a private physical therapy clinic.

If you can get even a quarter of the physical therapy clinics in your city as clients, and they keep coming back to you year after year because of your specialized knowledge, you'll be making more than enough money.

Let's take this very book as an example.

Who am I trying to bring value to? To men who have recently deconverted from their fundamentalist religion and want help trying to put their lives back together. That is my target niche market. I am *not* trying to also bring value to Christians. I am *not* trying to bring value to lifetime atheists whose lives are under control. I am *not* trying to bring value to deconverting women.

Because I have tightly defined who I'm targeting and trying to help—a very specific kind of customer—I can focus more clearly on how to reach and impact them.

It's okay if you struggle to identify a target market niche. I was surprised by how difficult it was for me to come up with a group of people to whom I could bring value and help solve their problems. After all, fundamentalists are all about helping and serving others, right?

The truth is that fundamentalists don't really help anyone in a practical way. They think they do, but they don't. Usually they'll find a group of people they suddenly decide they care about and then start praying for them.

A relative who needs to make a tough decision? Prayer.

A millennial friend who's going through a "tough time?" Prayer.

An unspoken prayer request from a visitor at the weekly Bible study? Prayer.

To them, the solution to every problem is to implore God for a few minutes to wave his magic wand and fix it. If he doesn't, then it must be God's will. Identifying and solving real-world problems is an entirely different skillset than what fundamentalists are equipped with.

Remember what I said in the section above about value? The more money someone is making, the more *real* value they must be bringing to many people. People who solve real-world problems with products and services get paid. Fundamentalists who pretend to solve real-world problems with prayer don't get paid and rarely have their prayers answered.

Step 3: Determine how you will solve your target market's problem.

You've figured out a target niche market, the problem they have, and the skill or knowledge you have that can solve that problem. Now determine *how* you will solve that problem.

Will you write a book, like me? Will you make videos? Podcasts? An app? A website? Maybe you need a physical product, in which case you will need to design it, find a manufacturer, build a prototype, test it, and trademark it. Or maybe it's a service you perform such as consulting or audio engineering.

Whatever you think will best meet the needs of your target market, do that. But you will also be more drawn to some strategies than others. Using myself as an example, I'm a writer, so my primary way of reaching my target market is through the written word. Maybe you don't like to write but you're a good communicator with an animated personality. Make a video! Or perhaps you're a hands-on guy who likes to tinker with gadgets and devices and likes cool and useful trinkets. Design a product.

In this step, you will also need to determine how much you will charge for your product or service. If you have a product, you obviously need to sell it for more than it costs you to manufacture and ship it—which will take some number-crunching. If you perform a service, you need to know how much time it takes you to perform the service and then charge accordingly based on how much you want to make per hour.

Assigning a monetary value to your product or service might make you uncomfortable. This is because your time in the Church likely taught you that value should be volunteered or given away for free. That *is* noble, but you need to unlearn that and remind yourself that you deserve to be paid for your time and effort. The value you give to your target market must be monetized. You need to make a living—literally.

Fortunately, most people *want* to pay for products and services they value because if they were free, eventually no one would provide them. If one day the high school kid you pay to mow your lawn told you that he's going to start doing it for free, you'd be happy—until he realized he needed the money and then decided to get another, better-paying job to make up for what he lost. Then you'd be stuck mowing your own lawn. Therefore you're happy to pay the kid to make sure he keeps doing the job you need him to do.

The same principle applies to your product or service. You can't keep bringing value to your target market if you don't charge them for it.

Step 4: Produce or Design the Product or Service that Will Solve Your Target Market's Problem

You've determined the best way to solve your target market's problem, and now you need to create it.

- If you are going to sell a book, you need to write it.
- If you are going to sell videos, you need to acquire video equipment and then produce the videos.
- If you are going to sell an app, you need to code it or hire someone else to code it.
- If you are going to sell a product, you need to research manufacturers and design the prototype.
- If you are going to perform a service, you need to determine precisely what you will do for your clients.

It's expected that this step can take many months. When you prepare something for sale, you want to take the time to get it right so that the customer, consumer, or client will have a positive experience. Remember the years of schooling and training you undertook to get the job (income source) you have now? It takes time to build an income source.

Step 5: Establish a Way to Get Your Product or Service into the Hands of your Target Market

Once you've finished creating what you plan to sell, you need a way for your target market to buy it from you.

If it's a product, it could mean setting up a website with a shopping cart program that accepts online payments directly into your bank account. It could mean selling on existing online marketplaces such as Amazon or Etsy. Perhaps you want to get your product stocked on the shelves of local retailers.

If it's a service, it usually means advertising to let your target market know that you are available to serve them. That could mean putting up some signs around your community. It could also mean establishing a social media presence dedicated to promoting the service you offer.

The best option is to choose whichever method (or methods) that makes it easiest for your target market to access, and then buy, your product or service.

Step 6: Design a Marketing Plan

Even if your new product or service is awesome, you won't make any money unless people in your target market know it exists.

Now is the time to unlearn all the humility and meekness from your fundamentalist days. It's time to be proud of what you've created and the way you are helping people in your target market. You've come this far to design something useful for people, so you should be excited—even if a little nervous—to get the word out.

This has nothing to do with being a sleazy salesman

who relies on tricks and concealed truths to sell things that don't actually help people. When you were a Christian, did you ever present the gospel to someone? Probably, and you likely did it often. In that moment, you were a sleazy salesman. You were trying to sell a solution that didn't work to someone who didn't have a problem that needed fixing.

Now you can sell a real, practical solution to someone who actually has a genuine need. And since you already have experience approaching random strangers, you have what it takes to pitch and sell. And since you've carefully chosen a target market, the prospects you present your product or service to will immediately see its value without you having to do much selling.

There are many different methods of advertising and they all work. Your job is to choose one or several and test them over time to determine which ones are most effective in reaching your target market and driving sales. Here are some examples:

- pay-per-click advertising
- social media advertising
- booking appearances on relevant podcasts
- running ads during YouTube videos
- running ads on your local television channels or radio stations

All of these methods are relatively easy to learn with a little time spent researching and practicing. If you choose to pay for your advertising, start with small amounts of money, especially if you've never done it before. Don't invest more into advertising until you've found a paid advertising strategy that generates sales profitably.

Step 7: Continue Marketing Your Product or Service

Telling people about your product or service never stops. Even Coca Cola spends billions on advertising every year, and everyone already knows what Coca Cola is. Fortunately, as you progress, a lot of this can be automated.

- Successful pay-per-click ad campaigns can be set to display continuously.
- Satisfied online buyers will write you good reviews, which essentially provides free advertising for you.
- Enthusiastic offline buyers will recommend your product or service through word-of-mouth referrals.

The great thing about an income source you own and control is that you can decide how much you want to earn from it. This is a big improvement from trying to increase your salary, where you need to hope that your boss agrees to it. And even if your boss is willing to pay you more, your boss's boss may not be.

For your product or service, you can literally raise the price whenever you want, instantly increasing your income. There are deeper business strategies to consider when doing this, of course, but you get the idea. *You* control the income. Not a boss. Not God.

You can keep the income source as a small business or

scale it larger if you think the potential is there. When it begins to generate enough money, you can even hire a business manager to oversee its operations while you sit back and collect the profits.

Now *that* sounds like freedom.

How Should Your Money Be Structured?

Let's say you've been inspired by the previous sections and implemented an action plan. Maybe it took you several years, but you changed your job, increased your income, and built additional sources of income that have made you financially more secure.

Now what? How should you structure your money?

I am not a financial advisor and you should talk to one before doing anything. I can, however, tell you how I structured my money with a strategy that has given me a peace of mind unlike any I've ever had.

Level 1: Put at Least $1,000 in an Emergency Cash Account

Remember what I said earlier about money being security? Unexpected things *do* happen. So scrape together a thousand dollars, open a separate bank account, put this money there, and don't touch it unless there's an emergency. If a sudden and unavoidable expense comes up, the money will be there to take care of it. That's what this account is for.

After the emergency has passed, replenish this account as fast as possible.

Level 2: No Debt

Once your emergency fund is established, the first thing you should do with any extra money is to pay off all your debt. Yes, all of it. No exceptions (except maybe your home, if you own one, and depending on whether or not you consider your mortgage to be "good debt").

Until you pay off your debt, there is no sense in doing anything else with your money because your debt accrues interest as time passes. This pointless hemorrhaging of your hard-earned cash will delay or even sabotage your financial security.

I even recommend that you stop contributing to any retirement or savings accounts and aggressively attack your debt instead. What's the point of putting money into a savings account that earns positive interest while the negative interest on your debt piles up? They don't just cancel each other out—negative interest always wins, which mean you lose.

Credit card debt. Student loan debt. Car loans. Pay them all off. Until you do this, you are not free. No one who owes money is free until they no longer owe.

> *Proverbs 22:7: "The rich rule over the poor, and a borrower is a slave to the lender."*

Sorry to drop a Bible verse on you in a book about deconversion, but some wisdom is just as true today as it was thousands of years ago.

Level 3: Have Six Months (12 is Better) Worth of Living Expenses in an Easily Accessible Account

This step comes after you have paid off all your debt and established an emergency account. Calculate your average monthly expenses (not income) and multiply that by six. Your goal is now to open *another* account and contribute excess savings to it until you have six months-worth of living expenses. This is in case you unexpectedly lose your job.

When times get tough, employer loyalties go out the window no matter how long you worked for them or how great of an employee you were. If you get laid off or your employer goes bankrupt, you need a safety net until you find another job.

Unexpectedly losing a job can be devastating, but if you can cover six months or more of your expenses, your life can proceed relatively smoothly until you find a new job.

Level 4: Earn a Monthly Income that Provides the Lifestyle You Want

You are now debt free and have a healthy cushion in case you lose your job. You should be resting pretty easy. Now comes the fun part. You've fixed the present and now you can start planning for a brighter future. It begins by asking yourself a key question:

What kind of lifestyle do I want and how much will it cost?

If you're a younger guy, this is a question you should ask yourself *before* deciding which college to attend or what to major in. If you're older, it's never too late to answer the question and make adjustments as needed.

People in the Church are *never* told to ask themselves this key question. Asking it suggests that we are in control of the answer rather than God, and the only thing that matters is obeying God's plan. When making big life decisions, we would often pray, "God, what is your plan for my life?"

You now know that none of that is true. Prioritizing God's plan over your own desires steals your life away with sometimes devastating results. Who would ever answer, "I want to make less than the median income, have tons of student loan debt, and be one emergency away from bankruptcy." And yet many people end up this way because they never had a chance to ask themselves the key question.

The deconverted man can now ask himself how he really wants to live, but it is vitally important to be honest. God isn't watching. Your men's group gets no vote. You can be selfish.

- Do you want to collect sports cars? Great. Look up how much each sports car you want costs and tally it up.
- Do you want to live in a suburban neighborhood with two kids and a mid-range car? Great. Calculate the approximate costs of that home, that car, and the kids. Don't forget to factor in the other expenses like insurance, schooling, and all the other necessities of life. The easiest way to do this is to find someone who lives this way and ask him about how much it costs in total.
- Do you want to travel the world with only

your possessions on your back? Great. Look up the cost of flights, currency exchanges, and on-the-ground costs of transportation, lodging, and food of the destinations you want to visit.
- Do you want six kids and to live in the country? Great. Look up the average amount of money it takes to raise a kid to age 18 and multiply that by six. Learn the average costs of houses in the area where you want to live. Again, the easiest way to do this is to find someone who lives this way and ask him about how much it costs in total.

Your calculations won't be dead-on accurate, of course, but you can get a ballpark idea of how much the life *you want* will cost you. Then you can figure out what job to take, what skills to learn, or what business to start in order to make the money you'll need. Equally as valuable, this figure will tell you which professions to avoid.

Once you know roughly how much you need to make per month, you can use the sections above to head toward that goal. Maybe you need to switch jobs or to gain new skills. Maybe you need to move to a new city where the pay is better. Maybe you need to build a few additional sources of income. You have six months of living expenses saved, so you are free to take some risks as you pursue what you desire.

Whatever amount of money per month you need to live on *your terms*, remember to add a little extra because you will also want to…

Level 5: Contribute to a Well-Balanced and Diversified Investment Portfolio

Church people view tithing as an investment. Give money to God and he will bless you later. It's the worst investment you could possibly make. You need to save for the future in a more practical way.

Money you allocate to a portfolio is money you should never touch until you can no longer work. This money is meant to take care of you in your old age. It's designed to do the job God was supposed to do back when you believed.

Specific advice regarding investments and stock portfolios is outside the scope of this book. You will need to do your own research. As a general recommendation, I suggest keeping your long-term investments in something reasonably safe and with a strong likelihood of a return, even if that return is small. It will add up over time.

If you want to be more aggressive and go for a high risk, high-reward return, do it with money you've set aside for that sole purpose. This should be an amount that won't negatively impact your financial standing if you lost it all. Treat that money the same as if you were taking it to the casino. If you win big, great. If you lose it, that sucks, but you're still okay.

Conclusion

We've covered a lot here. Money is an extensive and complicated topic and, in many ways, we haven't even scratched the surface.

Still, people who spend a majority of their life in the

Church usually get filled with many incorrect beliefs regarding money, financial security, and the relationship between money and happiness. When they are taught that God will take care of them and that money is inherently bad, they are living very dangerously as far as their future goes.

Leaving the Church does not immediately remove these false beliefs, but they need to be sorted out as soon as possible. In some cases, I'd argue that your financial situation should be the first thing you seize control of when you leave the fold.

When your money, investments, and income are handled, the peace of mind that comes with that is greater than any peace you could hope to get from a sermon, a worship song, or the Bible.

Chapter 6

YOUR HEALTH

"No man has the right to be an amateur in the matter of physical training. It is a shame for a man to grow old without seeing the beauty and strength of which his body is capable."
—Socrates

I once had a 65-year-old colleague who was quite the inspiration.

- He was in the gym every day, lifting way more weight than me.
- He ran marathons and completed triathlons.
- He played rugby with guys thirty years younger than him.
- He traveled the world.
- He jogged or biked home after a busy shift at work.
- He participated in Tough Mudder events—obstacle courses that put you through water, mud, ice baths, fire, and even electricity.

- He ate salads most days and rarely drank alcohol.
- He meditated daily.

As you can see, not your typical 65-year-old. After getting to know him, I decided I wanted to be as able as him when I reach his age. So I asked him for the secret behind his motivation. He shrugged and smiled.

"There is no secret. I've always been active. I can't *not* be active. If I don't get some type of exercise each day, I'll go crazy. People always think they can just stop when they get older. It's like they already have a predetermined age cutoff where they're allowed to start saying, 'I'm too old for that now.' But age is just a number."

It turned out, as it often does, that there really is no secret. It is simply a matter of doing what I already know I should be doing, which is to take care of my body and health because no one else will do it for me.

What the Church Teaches You About Health

In general, the Church misses the mark entirely regarding the health of your human, earthly body. You will often hear common reminders that "your body is a temple," but all that really means is don't get tattoos or excessive piercings and lock up your genitals until you're married.

The most absurd and dangerous sects of fundamentalism go so far as to prohibit potentially life-saving medical treatment such as blood transfusions. They attribute nearly all aspects of health to God.

Sickness or injury? God's plan.

Early death? God's plan.

Long life? God's plan.

Fundamentalists don't usually concern themselves with preserving their bodies or extending their lifespan because they are promised eternity in heaven so why bother? It's as if they want to fast forward through this life in order to get to the next one. They view the earthly body as a snakeskin to be shed or a vessel to be abandoned like a crab's shell.

The next time you shower, take a long look at your naked body in the bathroom mirror. See it for what it is—a construction of meat, bones, and blood but also a complex biological machine with thousands of processes running simultaneously, working on your behalf, every second of your life.

God did not create your body, God will not take care of your body, and God will not kill your body to further some aspect of his mysterious plan. Your body is yours and completely under your control. This is liberating, but it also comes with responsibility.

Your Health and Longevity Matter

"Dear Lord. I'm going through a busy season right now. I'm tired, fatigued, and sick. Please God, give me strength. I have so much to do."

How many times have you heard that prayer before? Probably in every Bible study you've ever attended. Perhaps you've even prayed this one yourself. Fundamentalists use this prayer or a similar one to assign God a homework assignment that he will never complete, the consequences of which are disastrous—not because he didn't finish the assignment, but because the responsibility for your health has been taken out of your hands.

There are literally no downsides to leveling up this aspect of your life. When you make yourself healthier, you will feel better, look better, perform better, and sleep better; you will have less stress, more focus, more mental clarity, better moods, and better sex; you'll get sick less often, sustain fewer injuries, and live a longer life.

Read back over that list one more time. All of that stuff is what fundamentalists around the world constantly pray for, then sit and wait for God to deliver. But not you. Not anymore. You are a man of action. You get off your ass to build a healthy lifestyle and a better body.

Maintaining Your Health Is a Lifestyle

You've probably heard that before: Diet and exercise as a way of life, not something you just do for a short period of time.

It's true.

When you decide to take the future of your health away from God, faith, and prayer and back into your own hands, you should also decide to make it something you do for the rest of your life. I mean that literally. Take care of your health *until the day you die*.

- It means you don't wait until you and your friends sign up for a 10k before you start training to run long distances.
- It means you don't wait for the office challenge to lose weight and win the pool.

- It means you don't make New Year's fitness resolutions that you forget about by February.
- It means you don't starve yourself before the holidays so you can binge Christmas dinner.
- It means that you are proactive and do a little bit each day, or every other day, and focus on long-term results.

That's the good news about making this a lifestyle rather than a temporary change. By engaging in physical activity for at least an hour each day or even every other day *until the day you die*, you will experience enormous benefits. Improvements in your health compound like money. Invest a fraction of a percent each day, and soon your returns are doubling and tripling.

Balanced Health

I'm of the opinion that every man should seek balance and avoid extremes. You don't need to be the strongest or to run the furthest or be the most ripped to get where you want to go. But you do need to be capable of performing basic physical actions when needed.

We men tend to hyper-focus on areas we're naturally good at or enjoy the most while disregarding the rest. This happens a lot in the fitness world. Some guys will become obsessed with bodybuilding and focus only on lifting weights. Others are into long-distance running and focus only on training for marathons.

What good is it to be able to lift three hundred pounds but not have the stamina to catch a leaving bus? What's the point of being able to run twenty miles without stopping but struggle to lift heavy furniture when moving into a new house?

Exceptions to this would be for those of you who play a sport which requires a certain type of fitness and training. For example, boxers need to be strong but without being bulky like a bodybuilder. If you are heavily involved in a sport, you still should analyze your lifestyle and identify any gaps in your health. Remember that your life will likely last longer than the time you spend participating in that sport.

Diet

No one needs to tell me that Doritos, Chicken McNuggets, and Cherry Coke are bad for me, which sucks because I love all of those things.

I do believe that most of us have good intentions about eating healthy. We also know how because a healthy diet isn't rocket science. Our excuses generally involve time and money. Time, because even though you know you should cook your own food at home, it can take up to an hour to fix a decent dinner, not including kitchen cleanup. Money, because high-quality food is expensive. Organic, locally sourced, naturally raised meat, fruit, vegetables, and other products are the best things to put inside your body but they cost more. There is really no way of getting around this fact.

Fitness and health expert Paul Chek often says, "Food isn't just fuel—it's information."

Think about that for a minute. God isn't maintaining your body with his grace and power. Your body is a walking mountain of cells that are growing, dying, shedding, and reproducing. When your cells reproduce, they don't just appear from nowhere like a Jesus miracle. They are built from the nutrients, the *information*, you put into your body.

Do you want your body to be informed and rebuilt by Red Bull, Cheetos, and the unpronounceable preservatives in your frozen pizza? Or do you want your new cells to be informed by water, vegetables, and protein?

This is why you feel better when you eat better. When you maintain a healthy diet, you are upgrading the quality of your cells. Which brings us back to the issue of affording all this stuff—and why I put the chapter on money before this one. If you first increase your income, you can increase your budget for healthy food. There is little point in trying to amend your diet unless you can afford to do it long-term and not just temporarily.

If you want to get your diet back on track before you secure additional income sources, start by simply *removing the bad* from your diet. Remember, removing the negative is just as powerful, if not more so, than adding the positive.

The easiest first step is to stop buying unhealthy beverages for your home such as soft drinks, sugary juices, and beer. When addressing their diet, most people tend to monitor what they eat and forget to monitor what they drink. You don't have to give them up completely—you can still have that stuff when you go out. Just keep them out of the house so you don't drink them every day. I also suggest weaning yourself off of sugar and cream in your coffee.

These simple cuts—and others you choose—will make a massive difference. After you've made these changes, repurpose the money you once spent on these items into buying higher-quality food.

If time is your limiting factor instead of money, utilize one of the many food prep companies that have shown up in the last few years. Most deliver healthy food that is conveniently packaged and can be brought to work each day. If you can't yet afford a food prep company, prepare a week's worth of food in one evening (such as a big soup), store some in glass containers, and then freeze the rest, thawing it as you need it.

Physical Strength

Men should be strong.

I don't mean transforming yourself into a macho bro with bulging muscles (although you can do that if it makes you happy). I mean that men should be able to lift heavy things within reason.

Since our caveman days, the tribe looked to men to build, fight, hunt, and produce. We aren't cavemen anymore but physiologically we haven't evolved much beyond where our ancestors were. Our primal male bodies respond positively when we build our strength.

Maybe that sounds old school and you're right; I'm a little bit old school when it comes to these things. But I also think a lot of men within the Church don't build their strength because they see it as a point of pride. God is supposed to be the powerful one, not us. Also, Jesus was meek, and we were taught that with God and Jesus on our side, we could be strong and powerful without literal physical strength.

Not true.

You don't need to be the strongest or most ripped guy in the world, but if you are physically weak, you will be a bit less healthy and a bit less happy. Fortunately, building strength is simple: not easy, but simple. You know the difference, right?

There are a couple of different ways that you can increase your overall strength.

Lifting Weights

Join a gym and focus on training that includes the four compound lifts: squat, deadlift, bench press, and overhead press. They are called compound lifts because they work the entire body, which makes them efficient for building total body strength. These lifts are performed with a barbell. Disregard exercising with machines and dumbbells when you first start out. They are usually modified or watered-down versions of the four compound lifts.

Although they may seem simple, these four compound exercises are quite complex. There's a lot going on inside your body when you perform them, especially with heavier weights. Make sure you spend some time researching form and technique before starting. Don't hesitate to ask someone who works at the gym to show you how to do them.

Learning and perfecting the four compound movements can (and should) take some time, but it's an investment worth making.

The internet is filled with workout programs designed to build strength. Some beginners favor "Starting Strength" by fitness coach Mark Rippetoe. That's the one I used when I first started out, and I got much stronger.

Don't forget to eat a lot of protein when you start lifting—meat, fish, and eggs. Remember the Paul Chek quote mentioned earlier. Food is information. Muscles are built from protein. If you lift heavy weights without also introducing protein into your diet, your body will have nothing with which to build new muscle cells.

Kettlebells

If you don't yet have the time to take on the four compound movements, kettlebells are a great tool for seeing rapid improvements in your fitness. Your gym should have a rack of them; they look like cannonballs with a handle and come in different weights. They are quite versatile and you can use them for a variety of unique movements.

The "kettlebell swing," for example, is one of the most powerful exercises you can do. There are plenty of how-to videos online or ask one of the instructors. If you do 100 kettlebell swings in however many sets it takes you, resting 60 seconds between each set, you will have gotten a decent, full-body workout in about twenty minutes. Do it every other day and you'll see quick improvement. You'll gain strength and endurance and lose body fat. When you get to where you can do 100 swings in only one or two sets, start using a heavier kettlebell. Track your results so you can see your progress.

Bodyweight Exercises

It's possible to become stronger without paying for a gym membership and with little equipment or none at all.

There are plenty of good bodyweight exercise routines available on the internet that can really whip you into shape. Most can be done with a minimum amount of gear and nothing you need to buy if you get creative enough. Push-ups, pull-ups, lunges, and bodyweight squats are just a few of the easily accessible options that can deliver great results.

That means there is almost no excuse for not improving your strength, starting today.

Endurance

On the other end of the spectrum, there's endurance. Being strong and ripped will do little good when you need to run through an airport to catch your flight. It's worth dedicating some of your workout time to increasing your endurance and conditioning and building a stronger, healthier heart. After all, the heart is the organ that keeps you alive.

Since you can't lift weights every day (and shouldn't), you can easily add endurance or cardio workouts between your weightlifting sessions.

The most basic option is to go for a jog every now and then. Set a distance goal and achieve it—the most popular and common seems to be 5K, which I agree is a doable distance for most guys to run. Use the app "Couch to 5K" for a simple running plan to get you there. If you nail it, then increase your goal to 10K.

After you build your endurance and can run for a reasonable distance, work on increasing your speed. Add sprints to build an explosive, short-distance running ability. They can also really get your heart going.

If you're one of those guys who hates running more than anything else in the world, you can build endurance in other ways. Swimming, jumping rope, rowing machines, and riding a bicycle are good alternatives.

Stretching

Most people consider stretching as something to be done before *real* exercise such as lifting weights or running. It's actually a lot more than that. A comprehensive, full-body stretching routine should be done even if you don't have time to do any other physical activity that day.

As you get older, your body will start getting stiffer and creakier. Older readers know what I'm talking about; you younger guys surely know some older folks who just can't get around as well as they used to.

Just like workout programs, stretching routines are a dime a dozen on the internet. Do some research and then schedule one into your day, ideally as one of the first things you do in the morning. I've begun doing this as a preventative measure.

If you prefer more direct guidance, consider joining a yoga class. There are probably dozens in your city every single day. Yoga is a great way to increase mobility and preserve your muscle and joint health—it can also be quite vigorous. You'll use muscles you never knew you had. An added bonus is that yoga classes can be a great way to meet some ladies…

Mental Health

Do not neglect your mind.

Taking care of your body will also spill over into your mental health because your mind and body are inextricably linked. However, if you suffer from mental or emotional stress, there is nothing wrong or shameful about seeing a therapist—ideally, a non-religious one.

If you can, try to reframe your mental health issues as a challenge you will eventually solve, not something you'll have to live with the rest of your life. As a deconverted man, it's highly likely that a lot of your mental health issues stem from your time spent in an abusive, fundamentalist environment. For years—perhaps your entire life—you were told:

- you aren't good enough on your own.
- you are inherently an evil sinner.
- your questioning and confusion could land you in hell.
- your good deeds are like filthy rags.
- your plans for your own life don't matter; only God's plan mattered.
- your natural inclinations and sexual desires are wrong, dirty, and sinful.

Frankly, breaking out of a fundamentalist religion without *any* lasting damage would be a Jesus miracle.

This book chooses to focus on practical methods for restoring your mental health. Doing, accomplishing, and working toward positive, meaningful goals can go a long way in healing your mind. And again, if you do feel like you can benefit from talking to a professional counselor as things come up for you while reading this book, please do so. There are also counselors who specialize in past religious trauma and spiritual abuse.

Sexual Health

Most of what I have to say about sex is covered in the chapter regarding your relationships with women. This section will discuss your sexual health, a topic that could fill an entire book, especially for recently deconverted men.

The Truth About Sex

Sex is a bodily function like digestion or waste elimination. It is how species reproduce. Humans also use sex to bond, show love and affection physically, and for recreation. It was not designed by God. It was not designed only for a married couple. It was not even designed to only occur between a man and a woman.

The reproductive system of your body is its own complex microcosm that needs to be taken care of instead of ignored or suppressed as the church has always preferred.

Barring a few rare exceptions, humans need sex regularly. Not having regular sex is detrimental to your overall health in many ways, such as:

- Increased risk of illness[1]
- Decreased tolerance for stress[2]
- Increased occurrence of erectile dysfunction[3]

And the list goes on. Therefore, as part of your overall health initiative, be sure to have regular sex. Gone are the days of suppressing your natural sex drive because your pastor told you to.

How often you have sex is up to you, but the key is to have it regularly. If you need it three times a week, then do it. If you need it once a month, do that instead. Just try not to resign yourself to a lower frequency if you need it more often. And be honest about your personal sex drive. Don't be the dumbass who brags to his friends, "Yeah, man, I need it twice a day every day! She'd better keep up!"

No. Listen to your body and experiment. Track how long it takes to start feeling the urge for sexual release. You know the feeling I'm talking about, and it's different for every guy.

If you're one of those guys who rarely or never feels sexual desire, then I'm sure your natural ability to resist sexual temptation worked in your favor during your fundamentalist days. Honestly, however, there is probably a deeper problem you need to address. Whether it's past trauma or low testosterone, you should see a physician and figure it out. Barring rare exceptions, it isn't normal to go through life without ever feeling sexual desire.

Masturbation

Masturbation is normal and healthy and something you should feel free to do without guilt or shame. There isn't much more to say about this because even people within the Church masturbate regularly no matter how much they pretend they don't.

Safe Sex

The modern-day Church is generally pretty tolerant of practicing contraception. There are, however, a few groups and sects that interpret certain verses of the Bible as condemning anything that blocks God's intended nature.

It is not a sin to prevent conception from happening. It is *your choice* and I encourage you to make it *every time* you have sex.

Raising a child is difficult, expensive, and time consuming. Fortunately, these days you have access to a variety of birth control methods that can help you prevent unintended pregnancies while still having sex. If Church-rooted guilt is clogging your brain about these methods, please get past it *before* having sex with anyone. The biggest victim of an unplanned, unexpected pregnancy is usually the child.

It's highly possible you never received sufficient sex education from your school or parents, and we could go on forever about how poorly the Church prepares people for having sex lives.

If you've deconverted and you're unmarried, then it stands to reason that your dating, relationships, and sex life will now take place in the context of the secular world rather than the sheltered bubble of the Church. That means you will be interacting with women who are more sexually experienced and sexually open than those you'll find in the pews.

As a man, you need to become familiar with condoms. If you aren't, buy a box and practice putting them on. This is a critical life skill. I know it sounds pretty basic, but you need to learn the correct way to use a condom before getting sexual with anyone.

Condoms are still the only widely accessible and affordable method of contraception that men can *control*. If you want to be sexually active but don't want a baby, then you need to be responsible for controlling your own contraception. You *cannot control* your partner's birth control pills or intrauterine devices (IUDs). Even the most disciplined, best-intentioned women occasionally forget to take their birth control pill. Two missed pills is sometimes all it takes.[4] And although rare, IUDs can malfunction and become dislodged.[5] Therefore, you should still wear a condom even if your partner tells you she's on birth control or has an IUD.

If you're dating in a secular context, it's likely that you will have sex with a new partner much sooner into the relationship than would ever happen in the Church. That means you and this girl won't yet know each other that well. This is fine and not a sin, but you should still take reasonable precautions until you two know each other better.

If your new partner is using birth control pills or has an IUD, it's possible she will tell you that you don't need a condom because she has it covered. Whenever you hear this, remember this important truth:

Her being on birth control does not take away your right to choose safety and protection for your body.

Be strong and insist on protection. She may get upset. She may accuse you of not trusting her. She's right. You shouldn't trust anyone fully in such important matters until you get to know them better. Do you really want to be with a woman who doesn't care about your own sense of sexual safety? Besides avoiding an accidental pregnancy, condoms are also more effective at preventing sexually transmitted diseases whereas female birth control is not. If you find yourself in such a situation, politely and respectfully end the encounter.

If you haven't already, spend some time researching sexually transmitted diseases. The most common ones are chlamydia, gonorrhea, and herpes. They aren't running rampant as the Church wanted you to believe, but they are definitely out there and you *do* need to know the signs and how to protect yourself.

Testosterone

Men are the way we are because of testosterone. This hormone makes us (women as well, though men have a lot more of it naturally) stronger, more muscular, more assertive, more energetic, more focused, more ambitious, and more sexually driven.

I encourage every man reading this to go to a lab or clinic in your city, get your blood drawn, and find out where your testosterone levels are (I did). This is especially important if you struggle with low energy or tend to be sluggish in your day-to-day life. Abnormally low testosterone could be one of the reasons.

Testosterone does decrease as you get older, which is something else to keep an eye on as you age. However, don't passively accept your doctor's observation that lower testosterone levels are normal for older men. While true, they don't have to stay that way;[6] you can naturally boost them by doing some of the things mentioned earlier in this chapter while adding a few others:

Lift Heavy Weights[7]

The compound lifts discussed earlier will serve you well for boosting testosterone because they are heavy, full-body movements. But be careful; there's a threshold above which more is *not* better, so don't overtrain. Overtraining can actually *decrease* testosterone.

Eat Meat

Red meat is typically best (because it contains zinc, which is necessary for testosterone production). Other foods that will boost your testosterone are eggs, bacon, and beans.[8]

Get Good Sleep[9]

During sleep, testosterone forms along with many other reparative bodily processes. When you don't get enough sleep, you narrow the window of opportunity for your body to take care of itself. Aim for seven to eight hours per night.

Take Zinc[10] and Magnesium[11] Supplements

These two minerals are integral for testosterone development. You can buy them in pill form.

Reduce Stress[12]

I know it's easier said than done, but find ways to lower your stress levels.

Get Vitamin D3[13]

When you get your blood drawn to check your testosterone, also check your levels of vitamin D3. If you don't get enough sunlight, this value will be low and you'll need to take a supplement—or get out into the sun more often.

Have Sex[14]

If you're an unmarried guy abstaining from sex because Jesus told you to, I have some good news for you: Testosterone increases when you have sex.

As a man, everything about your mood, energy, and performance gets better when you have optimal testosterone levels. So check your levels regularly and stay active!

Conclusion

One life. One body. One chance.

It can take a while to fully realize that God did not create your body nor will he take care of it for you. Fortunately, thanks to science, we know more about how the human body works than we ever have in human history. Further, we have access to tools and knowledge to care for our bodies and health in ways that were unavailable to the generations that came before us.

Reclaiming your health from God is one of the most therapeutic ways to practically move on from a life lived in fundamentalism. Always remember that you must care for yourself *first* before you can truly take care of others.

Chapter 7

YOUR FAMILY

"A family is a risky venture, because the greater the love, the greater the loss... That's the trade-off. But I'll take it all." — Brad Pitt

Like most "houses of worship," Sundays at my church were attended predominantly by families: a couple and their two or three kids. The kids would head upstairs for Sunday school and the parents would attend the sermon. Sometimes they would even dress similarly. This was most apparent on Easter when the entire family would come wearing various bright, pastel colors.

Everything in everyone's lives seemed perfect. Or, at least, they all put on a convincing performance that everything was fine when they were at church.

I remember one Sunday when I'd arrived at church early and had taken my seat. I had time to watch as these idealistic church families filed in for their weekly sermon. Perhaps I was in a bad mood that day, but a grim thought popped into my head out of nowhere: What would happen if a member of that perfect family—whether the man, the woman, or one of the kids—suddenly decided they no longer believed in God?

That poor family would go into a tailspin.

It would upset the status quo. It would rock the boat. Their tidy, picturesque family image would shatter. The person who left the faith would be regarded as someone who'd developed a terminal illness. The family would be pitied. They'd be the target of prayer requests in Bible study groups throughout the church.

The worship music started, ending my depressing thoughts before they could go further. But years later, as I listened to many deconversion stories, I was often reminded of my negative thoughts on that particular Sunday morning. What I had day-dreamed had become a reality for most of those who had deconverted. The horrified reaction from their families, and the subsequent fallout, proved to be one of the most difficult aspects of their deconversion.

What the Church Teaches You About Family

The grimmest teaching regarding your family comes right from the mouth of Jesus. In Luke 14:26, he says, "If anyone comes to me and does not hate father and mother, wife and children, brothers and sisters—yes, even their own life—such a person cannot be my disciple."

However, you'd be hard-pressed to find a church in the Western world that interprets this literally. Usually, it's presented as an exercise in comparison—that your love for God should be so strong as to make your love for your earthly family resemble hate, even though it's actually love.

That's confusing, right? I think this is yet another verse that makes the Bible look bad and that churches need to regularly spin in a more palatable direction.

Despite this verse, churches tend to place a huge emphasis on the family unit. To them, there is nothing better than a portrait-ready family showing up to church together, worshipping together, and growing spiritually together. For young adult men and women in the congregation looking to marry, it's an ideal that drives them forward and gives them something to strive for.

So when someone deconverts and leaves the church, it can have a devastating impact on the members of that person's family. The father will feel as if he has failed at being the spiritual head of the household. The mother will wonder if there was something she could have done differently. Brothers and sisters will be shocked and confused.

On the other hand, if the man who deconverts already has his own family, he may feel regret for teaching his kids beliefs that he no longer holds. He may wonder if his wife, who married him under the pretense of building a Christian family, will feel deceived and betrayed.

In extreme cases, a family may react to a deconversion as if that person had unexpectedly passed away.

Any of these scenarios presents a huge complication in a man's deconversion process. His friends are easier to lose because he can make new, more like-minded ones in his new life, but his family cannot be replaced.

Further, the deconverted man will still love his family regardless of them remaining in the religion. He has no desire to hurt them or make them feel guilty. But because of the fierce "you're in or you're out" nature of religion and the Church, the family can feel hurt and betrayed no matter how thoughtfully the deconverted man handles the situation.

These potential realities can culminate into one of the biggest and most difficult moments of a deconversion: Telling your family that you no longer believe.

Your Family and Your Happiness

Your family is likely a massive part of your life. Whether it's your parents or siblings or if you are the parent or all the above, much of your happiness will be derived from your family. If there is conflict, you will be less happy. If you have strong familial bonds, you will be happier.

Fundamentalist religion is only one of many factors that affect the quality of a family, but when one or more members of a family deconvert, the result can be catastrophic. That will be the focus of this section. Countless other factors affecting familial happiness have nothing to do with religion, but those are outside the scope of this book.

Families Are Complicated

This book aims to be a practical guide to life after deconversion. However, because everyone's family and familial situation is unique, it can't begin to cover the multitude of specific circumstances and their solutions. What I can do is suggest a general approach to handling your family post-deconversion and hopefully it will inspire some ideas for how to adapt these practices to your specific family dynamic.

First, I will discuss how to tell your family that you've deconverted—or if you should even tell them at all. Of all the people I've spoken to regarding these issues, telling their families that they no longer believe has been the biggest obstacle.

Don't Tell Your Family Until You Are Independent

One blanket statement for all deconverted men that I am comfortable making is this:

Do not tell your family that you've deconverted until after you are completely independent from them.

If telling them evokes a strong emotional reaction such as anger, then you need to have logistics in place to put some space between you and your family until things settle down.

Whatever you depend on your family for, they can take it away and withdraw their support. You may think it's ridiculous for your family to "punish" you in this way but remember that this is going to be an emotional situation, not a logical one. Emotions are far more unpredictable. You need to be prepared as best you can.

- If you're a high school student still living under your parents' roof, don't tell them yet.
- If you're a college student who depends on your parents to pay your tuition, don't tell them yet.
- If you're in your early twenties and have your own job and money and car but still live at home for convenience or to save money until

you get a place of your own, don't tell them yet.
- If you're completely independent, on your own two feet, and do not rely on your family's financial or logistical support—including incidental things such as occasionally borrowing their car—you can consider telling them that you've deconverted.

These guidelines can essentially be broken down by age, since the older you get, the more independent you become as you start to get your life in order. So if you're still in high school or just starting college, grit your teeth, nod and smile, go to church when you must, and be patient. Your life will be a whole lot easier if you can keep a lid on things until you're older.

The Option of Never Telling Your Family

You do have the option to *never* come clean with your family about your deconversion. If you live far away, for example, and only see them a couple of times a year, it's possible that your family will never notice your lack of church attendance or that you no longer listen to worship music or that you've stopped praying before you eat.

This could be ideal. You never have to rock the boat. But I know this tactic won't sit right with a lot of guys.

If you're the kind of man who can't keep this secret inside or feel that you're living a lie by not telling your family and the stress of it burdens you, then yeah, you will have to eventually let the cat out of the bag. Your own peace of mind takes precedence here, even if it means delivering an emotional blow to your religious family.

Don't Ask, Don't Tell

It's possible that you find yourself in a "Don't ask, don't tell" situation. This is where your family, knowing you well and being perceptive, will notice your slow departure from the church or changes in your behavior even though nothing is explicitly said out loud.

If you sense this is true, keep it that way. A surprisingly high number of people are okay with "Don't ask, don't tell" and your family might qualify. An analogous example of this is an older guy who refuses to see a doctor for a check-up, explaining that, "If there's anything wrong, I just don't want to know about it."

Respect "Don't ask, don't tell." Stating the truth out loud when your family would rather keep it unspoken will disturb the peace they've been able to make with your deconversion.

Families Suck at Keeping Secrets

Maybe you've already come out to a trusted sibling or a cool uncle. That's great. It's a step in the right direction, and this person may be able to help guide you when it comes time to tell the family members who will take the news the hardest.

But if you're in this situation, you should work toward doing the deed sooner rather than later. This is because even the trusted family member who knows about your deconversion can slip up. One careless word or comment to the wrong person at the wrong time could unleash an emotional storm.

You don't want the sensitive family members finding out from anyone who isn't you.

No one likes hearing big news—good or bad—from a third party. You've probably been in this situation before. Remember how it made you feel unimportant or as if you were an afterthought? You don't want your family to feel like this, even though the news you're delivering isn't good. It will just make everything harder than it's already going to be.

So if someone knows who could potentially give it away by accident, you need to finish the job. The more people who know, the quicker you need to tell your family yourself.

Preparing to Tell Your Family that You've Deconverted

Keep in mind that it's impossible to accurately predict how your family will react when you tell them you no longer believe. Even if you know them really well, proceed with caution. As I've said, emotional situations are full of wild cards.

I also need to reiterate an earlier point because it's that important: *If you aren't fully independent from your family yet, you should not be planning to tell them.*

When preparing to make the announcement, I highly recommend sitting down and writing out what you want to say. Schedule some dedicated time to do this that is free from distractions. Turn off your cell phone!

Writing promotes clear thinking. It also provides

many other benefits that you don't get from improvising a speech. You can scratch out, rewrite, clarify, or start over. You can also prepare your thoughts more slowly than risk speaking aloud and off the cuff.

Practice saying what you've written in front of a mirror. Record yourself if you want. Run through it with a friend who has also deconverted or post what you've written on a supportive deconvert internet forum or social media group.

You certainly aren't the first person to travel down this road. Seek advice and wisdom from those who have gone before you.

How to Tell Your Family that You've Deconverted

Imagine that you are telling your family a piece of big news, whether good or bad. How would you tell them, for example, that you are going to be a father or are moving far away to take a new job or that you'd just been diagnosed with a terminal illness? You would probably do it by scheduling a time to sit down face-to-face and have a dedicated discussion. The same principles apply here.

Set aside some time that isn't too short or too long. An in-person conversation is best, but if you live far away, do it over a video messaging app like Skype or Zoom. If you wrote out what you want to say, don't be afraid to read it to them straight off the paper. Even presidents addressing the nation read from prepared speeches. Alternatively, you can give it to them as a letter. If you do, make sure that you are present to continue the conversation after they read it, but don't let the discussion carry on for too long.

Whatever you say (or write if you choose to give them a letter), keep it succinct. You could simply say something along the lines of, "I no longer consider myself a Christian, and it's important that you know." Be nice and empathetic. Even if you are still in the anger phase of your deconversion, this is not the time to throw your parents' religious beliefs in their faces.

The biggest and most difficult question your family will likely ask is, "Why?" However your deconversion came about, though, this isn't the time to go into it. Don't talk about how you found inconsistencies in the Bible and no longer believe in the inerrancy of Scripture. Don't talk about watching Christopher Hitchens videos and being convinced. Don't talk about unanswered prayers or miracles that didn't happen.

The reason not to get into all this is because your family will feel like you are telling them that what they believe is wrong—look no further than politics to see how inflamed this can get. Find a way to communicate your decision without making them feel defensive. Something like, "It just doesn't really make much sense to me anymore," answers their question while also being vague. More than likely, though, they will persist. If one of your family members is well-versed in Christian apologetics, for example, you may find yourself in a religious debate or argument and this is not the time or the place.

Keep your finger on the pulse of the conversation. There will come a point when the information has been delivered and the message has been received but the grief or shock or disappointment will keep your family going with inconsequential questions (to you, though, not to them).

"But what about this?"
"But what about that?"
"Aren't you worried about—"
"How will you—"

If you feel they are going in circles and grasping at straws, it's time to exit. Say something like, "I have to go soon. The important thing was that you needed to know and that I told you the truth. If you have any more specific questions, we can talk about them later."

This allows the emotions to ebb and gives your family time for the truth to sink in. If they took it hard, give them time to come to terms with what you've told them. Other important details you should communicate include the following:

- Tell them this doesn't change the fact that you love them.
- Thank them for introducing you to their religion (if they did) and for all of the positive influences it had on you and how you were raised.
- Remind them that you are not rejecting them; they are still your family.

How to Deal with the Fallout

The ideal situation after telling your family about your deconversion is that they accept it with few problems or hurt feelings and everyone moves happily on. But if that were typical, this section wouldn't need to be written. Here's a list of the most common responses to a deconversion and how to handle them.

They Sadly Accept the Truth

Although it's unfortunate that you hurt your family, at least the truth is out and everyone knows. Continue to be kind, gentle, and empathetic.

They Are Angry

It's time to evacuate the premises. Quickly and politely end the discussion and leave. Spend some time apart and let the anger blow over.

They Temporarily Disown You

This is very unfortunate but it could happen. Give your family time and space and let them decide when to eventually reach out and break the silence.

They Permanently Disown You

This is highly unlikely. It takes a lot of work—logistical and emotional—to permanently disown a family member. However, if this happens to you, do whatever it takes to handle the emotions or trauma that comes. Strongly consider professional therapy.

They Become Resentful or Passive-Aggressive

I saved this one for last since it's the most common outcome. You may find over time that a lot of general negativity leaks out at family gatherings. Usually this will be in the form of passive-aggressive comments about atheists or nonbelievers. I recommend tolerating this for a while if the news of your deconversion is relatively fresh. Remember, they too deserve a phase for their anger and grieving.

If it persists, then it's time for some tough love. Tell your family you understand that what you told them was difficult, but you don't appreciate the negativity and it's time to let it go. Make it clear that if they don't stop, you won't be seeing them for a while and then follow through if they don't come around. Pick a specific timeframe for cutting off contact. Be strong. Don't answer calls or respond to texts.

When you reengage with them, don't talk about the break. Speak to them as if it never happened. Your family will know why you went radio silent and that their behavior caused it. This is a good exercise in respecting and enforcing your boundaries.

If the negativity continues, repeat the process.

How to Handle Your Own Family

If you have your own family (wife and kids), you'll have to deal with them as well, and no one solution fits all situations. It will depend on how old your kids are and how you raised them regarding religion. It also depends on your spouse's current stance on religion and the strength of your relationship. There are numerous combinations and it's impossible to address them all within this book.

However, I can suggest a few basic strategies to get you pointed in the right direction.

Your Spouse

I will cover your spouse or partner in the context of deconversion in the section regarding your relationships with women.

Younger Children

If your children are younger, then how you handle the situation will largely be up to you. I'm in no position to tell a parent how to raise their young child.

If you have indoctrinated your young child, you'll have to play the long game. And by indoctrination, I mean that you have done things such as:

- explicitly taught them about God, Jesus, the resurrection, and the gospel.
- instilled in them the importance of attending church every Sunday.
- read Bible stories before bed every night
- sung Christian children's songs together
- sent them to Vacation Bible School every summer

As a transition, read those Bible stories every other night and substitute "normal" stories on "off" nights. Increase the frequency of those non-Bible stories over time. You can also skip church occasionally if your spouse is supportive. Begin broadening the scope of your discussions on religion. By that, I mean presenting Christianity as one of many world religions and that non-believers aren't necessarily wrong or bad.

At this point, your young child may begin to ask some questions. He or she may ask why you've stopped going to church or why you don't read the Bible to them as much anymore. Your best bet here is, like everything else, the truth. A big theme of this book has been to live honestly according to *your* new truth, and the same can be said here.

You can honestly tell your young child that you've changed your mind and heart and that grownups do that sometimes.

Your young child may be confused, upset, or disappointed. It may be hard to put your young child through these uncomfortable emotions, especially if you feel responsible, but they will be temporary. Telling the truth also resolves the situation faster than dancing around the topic with avoidance.

I'd also suggest you emphasize teaching your young child how to think for himself and come to his own conclusions rather than trying to force him or her into following you into non-belief. Critical thinking and forming opinions is an essential life skill that will serve your young child well throughout his or her life, even beyond the scope of deciding what religion, if any, to follow.

If your child's other parent is still a believer and wants to continue raising your young child in the religion, then that, of course, is a discussion you'll need to have with your partner. Rather than having two warring factions, frame the mixed-faith family as yet another opportunity for your young child to experience multiple perspectives and make an autonomous decision. Spin this positively; explain to your young child that some people believe different things but that doesn't change the fact that you are all still a loving family.

Again, I am in no position to tell someone how to raise their young child. But if you've deconverted after you've indoctrinated your young child, it seems reasonable that you would not want to start indoctrinating your young child all over again with an atheist or agnostic worldview. Rather, it is best to give your child what you may have never had—the opportunity to think for his or herself.

Older Children

If your children are older (teenage years and above), you can approach them with a similar method to the one I described earlier in this chapter regarding telling parents you've deconverted. However, you won't be able to hide from them for long. Your kids will notice and won't be afraid to ask what's going on with you.

For this reason, it's in your best interest to initiate the conversation with them very soon after you realize that you need to come clean. When it comes to older children, what you say is important, but how you behave is perhaps even more important. When you proactively sit them down for this difficult discussion, it shows strength and boldness. You don't want to meekly confess after being cornered by your assertive teenager who's demanding an answer.

If your older children only went to church because you forced them to, they'll likely be relieved. If they are deep in the fold, however, they will likely become upset. As you did with your parents, remind your children that you will always love them no matter what they believe. And when you say that, mean it. Don't stir up drama by trying to exorcise all religion from your household. Don't become the belief police because you are going through an angry phase.

The bright side to this is that, unlike your parents, your older children may follow in your deconversion footsteps. This, of course, is dependent on a supportive spouse that doesn't want to enforce specific beliefs on your kids. Your children's beliefs were probably heavily influenced by you in the first place, and if you proceed with honesty and integrity, they'll see that losing your religion has left you unchanged or maybe even better. They will naturally emulate you.

Conclusion

Although it can happen, it's rare for older people (age 50 or so and above) to adopt new routines or lifestyles. We've all had a good laugh at grandpa who still insists on doing things (or thinking about things) the "old-fashioned way." Older people often hold on to their religious beliefs more tightly than their habits or flip phones. This way of life and thinking has served them for decades and they aren't interested in a change no matter how much evidence is presented.

Remember this when dealing with your own family. Once the hard part is done, just let it be. Don't try to change them. If they ask questions and follow you down your deconversion path, great. But trying to get your older parents to change at this point in their lives likely won't work.

If you have a family of your own, however, it's possible you may see a lot of change. Do your best to keep it positive. Get through any hurt feelings and disappointment as quickly as you can and shift into rebuilding.

When you show your children—young or old—how an honest adult changes his mind in the face of convincing evidence, you are teaching them how to think for themselves and be stronger individuals.

Chapter 8
YOUR SOCIAL LIFE

"A man's growth is seen in the successive choirs of his friends."
—Ralph Waldo Emerson

When I served in the youth ministry at my church, the other youth leaders became my core group of friends. They were all white, Christian, and heterosexual. We were all members of the same church, heard the same sermons, believed the same doctrines, attended the same weekly Bible study, participated in the same church events, and had the same objective: to evangelize the city's youth.

This was one of the happiest periods of my life. Because of my association with this fine group of people, I considered myself to be growing spiritually and as a person. It turned out I was wrong. There was a huge, diverse world out there I had yet to see and learn from. And while I never explicitly thought it, I subconsciously knew that introducing any kind of diversity or alternative ideal would cause problems.

One of the youth leaders would habitually remind the youth kids of an oft-repeated saying: "Your friends influence the quality and direction of your life." He said it as a way to encourage them to make good decisions about the company they chose to keep. I always nodded along. I never once thought to turn that statement back onto myself. I thought I was good to go, that my friends were influencing my life in a positive direction.

But were they? Yes and no.

They helped me to remain obedient to Church dogma, but in reality, did little to help me grow as a citizen of this world.

Growth occurs from being exposed to new ideas, challenges, and risks.

Growth occurs when you discover that you don't have the full truth like you once thought you did.

Growth occurs when you come to realize that the world operates as it does, not how you or others would like it to.

That is why I didn't grow while surrounded with these people, as nice and well-meaning as they were. They repeatedly confirmed my own limited worldview, providing a solid structure to my bubble. That's why it was one of the happiest times of my life—because it was easy. I was rarely challenged and never had to feel like I was wrong.

This was my social life from age 18 to about 22. I liked it then, but ultimately realized I was living in a cocoon and started asking myself if there was a better way.

As you read further, keep in mind that we are discussing friendships with other men.

What the Church Teaches You About Your Social Life

The Church doesn't explicitly tell you not to have friends outside the Church, but it does give you plenty of warnings that lead you to believe this. The most common was that non-believing friends would lead you into temptation and sin. Over time, you may have begun to see these people as hidden enemies, watching from shadowy corners, waiting for the perfect moment to steal your soul with alcohol, cigarettes, drugs, or sex.

In reality, people don't act or think this way. Non-believers are happily living their lives while they ignore the Church completely. Meanwhile, the people within the Church spend tons of time thinking about how "dangerous" non-believers supposedly are. Those more mature in their faith view non-believers as projects they need to convert and save from an eternity in hell. The Church supports this outside pursuit of non-believers and often uses the common refrain to "be in the world, not of the world."

Diving deeper down, we come to the topic of men's groups. Most churches have them. Their goal is structured male fellowship time. The practice is not inherently bad, and in fact can produce some good results. Men coming together in this way has happened throughout human history in all cultures and faiths.

Ideally they mix younger men with older men, which is intended to benefit the growth and development of the next generation. The gatherings are usually centered around traditional masculine activities such as sports, outdoors, and manual work. This is also a strong positive.

As usual, when the Church has a good idea, they execute it poorly or at best, sub-optimal.

One main problem with men's groups in churches is that they are too homogenous. All the men in the group go the same church, know the same people, and have the same belief system. Often, the members are of the same race and income class. You end up with a group of men who come together looking to grow, but since they are all carbon copies of each other, everyone ends up staying the same. The younger guys become clones of the older ones.

These groups are also heavily involved in "accountability." Sometimes they will shirk masculine "fun time" in favor of meetings that focus only on accountability. These men will meet once a week to confess how they have failed to adhere to the arbitrary and artificial standards of the Church. Usually, this results in a group of middle-aged men lamenting about how they looked at porn that week or how they struggle to "bounce their eyes" when the lady next door takes her morning jog around the neighborhood.

These conversations are not beneficial because they are based in shame and failure. What's worse, the actions (or inactions) they consider failures aren't actually failures. Your mind, body, and biology are programmed to draw your eyes to the neighbor lady when she takes her morning jog. That's just how it is.

When these groups urge members toward success and victory, it's again according to the arbitrary and artificial standards of the Church. Volunteering more time to the Church, tithing more money to the Church, or being content with what "God has given you" (translation:

settling for a life that doesn't fully satisfy you) are common goals.

How to Handle Old Church Friends

Most deconverted men automatically remove their old church friends from their lives. This a mistake. You've invested a lot of time with these guys. You likely share many fond memories of a part of your life you experienced together. Give these relationships a chance.

In your newly deconverted life, you are hopefully open-minded enough to be friends with Muslims, Buddhists, and everyone in between. Can't you also be friends with Christians?

Instead of immediately shutting Church people out of your life, a better approach is to stay connected to some of them based on certain conditions. Not everyone will, or can be expected to, respond to your deconversion the same way. Here are some suggested guidelines for choosing who to keep in your life and who to let go:

- If a friend prefers that you remain a Christian but is still able to talk to you and be friends regardless of your differing belief systems and doesn't try to change your mind, then it's okay to keep interacting with him.
- If a friend stops responding to your calls and texts and invitations to hang out, then you can rest better knowing that you tried to maintain the relationship and that the other person was the one unable to look past your differing beliefs.

- If a friend continues to be nice to you but is unable to interact without trying to convince you to change your mind, then firmly inform him that your decision is final. If he continues, then gently cut that person out of your life. Chances are that this friend will eventually stop talking to you anyway because he will never accept your deconversion.
- If a friend turns verbally or emotionally abusive or hostile, cut that person out of your life immediately. Examples of this would be unsolicited calls, texts, or social media posts that condemn you for your apostasy or choices.
- If you consider yourself traumatized by your experiences in your old church, then cut off all communication from everyone associated with that church. Trauma could be defined as physical abuse, sexual abuse, emotional abuse, gaslighting, manipulation, or a combination of these.

It's very possible that your deconversion has left you with few remaining friends. The deeper you were in your religion, the more likely this will be the case. You can remedy this by putting in some work on your social life like any of your other life areas.

The Natural Narrowing of Your Social Life

There's another phenomenon that deserves mention. It happens to most people whether or not they belong to a fundamentalist religion: the natural narrowing of your social life as time goes on.

As you grow older, you'll notice that friends and acquaintances fall away. All the time you spent hanging out with them gets replaced by other responsibilities such as your career, your family, and your kids. Likewise, your friends will start focusing on these things as well, making it harder and harder to get together.

This happens to almost everyone and is considered normal. But just because something is normal doesn't mean it's good.

The natural narrowing of your social circle from college and beyond *can* be a positive thing. As your life develops, you simply don't have the time to keep up with every casual acquaintance. That's fine. What isn't fine is allowing good friends and relationships—the guys who are worth keeping in your life—to fall by the wayside. Make every effort to keep them around.

The good thing is that most male friendships don't need much to keep them alive. Sometimes hanging out once a month is enough. Another good thing is that most male friendships are easily resurrected. If you realize that too much time has passed (even years) since the last time you connected with a guy you wish was still in your life, reach out. Make a plan to grab a beer. Guys bounce back fast, so take advantage of that.

Why You Need A Supportive, Quality Social Life

A combination of losing friends during deconversion and the natural narrowing of your social circle as you grow older can lead you to incorrectly think that you don't need many friends anymore. This isn't true.

"You are the average of the five people you spend the most time with."

Most people have heard this quote, which is commonly attributed to motivational speaker Jim Rohn. A difficult challenge may underlie this quote. Maybe your five best friends are truly great guys but are living below their potential. Maybe they have dreams and goals that they've put on hold and their inaction is influencing your own inaction.

So the question becomes, What average do you want? This quote suggests that it's important to examine who's in your life and that maybe these five great guys shouldn't be receiving the majority of your time.

One of the most quoted bits of wisdom in the Bible is that iron sharpens iron (Proverbs 27:17). In Bible times, a sharp blade was used to sharpen a dull blade until both were sharp. The analogy demonstrates how a mediocre man learning from a great man eventually becomes a great man as well.

This is still true even after you've deconverted. As I've said before, the Bible *is* right sometimes. It's the modern Church that distorts it.

Humans, especially men, rub off on each other. No man has become who he is in a vacuum. A blackbelt in karate didn't become so by himself. He was trained by a guy and he's competed against hundreds more to reach that level of success. An award-winning filmmaker first worked under other accomplished filmmakers and studied thousands of films made by others. A wealthy business owner got to where he is by putting his head together with other business owners to figure out what led to their success and how to build a long-lasting company.

Growth happens through challenge. When you try something and fail, you don't usually make that same mistake again the next time you try it. When you become really good at something, it no longer challenges you and so you will no longer grow, potentially leading to stagnation and boredom.

It is the masculine condition to be continuously challenged, and thus to continuously grow. This is why it is so important to focus on and nurture your social life. Your group of friends, if carefully sought out and selected, allows you to spend time with other quality men who can help you grow into a better version of yourself.

I think a big mistake a lot of men make is that they consider their social life merely as entertainment; their friends are an option when they're bored or have nothing to do that particular night. While friends are certainly entertaining, there is a lot missing from this mindset.

A social life that is chosen *by you* with great care and careful reasoning has the capability to elevate your life in ways that you never thought possible. It's not about "having friends in high places" (although that certainly helps) but rather having friends that are already better than you in ways that you would like to emulate. Spending time with these guys is truly a situation of iron sharpening iron.

This concept of iron sharpening iron also works in the reverse. Playing online shooter computer games for six hours is easier when you have buddies who are willing to do the same. If no one you know ever goes to the gym, it's harder develop a gym habit. If your friends still work at the same low-paying restaurant job three years after graduating college, you, too may not feel any urgency to seek something better. If some of the guys in your life are slowing you down, unmotivated, negative, or encouraging unhealthy habits, it may be time to move on.

How to Make New Friends

If you were in the Church for a long time, it's possible you don't know any other way to make friends or figured out how men become friends in the first place.

Making friends in the Church is easy. There is a strong connection based on shared beliefs and lifestyles. Outside the Church, things get a bit messier. You're faced with people who have unique lives and belief systems. Is it even possible to be friends with someone who is completely different from you?

The good news is yes. Men are deep and complicated creatures, but the way men bond is actually quite simple. There is a practical way to purposely seek out new guys to hang out with.

Down to the Pub

I can't explain it, but there is something about men that draws them to drink together. In some countries and cultures, it's not unusual for men to get together for a drink or two every evening.

So head to a local tavern, sit at the bar, and have a beer, maybe two. Preferably there's a male bartender. Make idle chitchat with him when possible but don't distract him when he's in the middle of something. If you do this a couple of times a week, you'll eventually become "a regular." Over time, you'll notice the other regulars and they'll notice you. Greet those guys every time you see them.

Over time, these friendly exchanges will naturally turn into conversations. Pretty soon you'll have a few strong acquaintances. Accept the first event they invite you to. If those don't come fast enough for you, put together your own event and invite them yourself.

Learn Something New

An even better method to make friends is to choose a hobby or skill you want to learn and find a class where it's taught. Examples include a sports club, a boxing gym, or a language learning class. Men bond quickly when doing such things together, especially traditionally masculine activities that include sports or anything outdoors.

Using this method brings additional rewards as well—you make new friends over a shared interest *and* improve your life by adding a quality hobby.

Honesty and Authenticity

However you choose to rebuild your circle of male friends, remember the key: be honest and authentic. No matter how introverted and private you are (I'll bet you aren't more introverted and private than me!), you need to open up and allow people to get to know you and your thoughts and feelings about the world around you.

This has always been a struggle for me. Some of the guys in my life who I consider to be close friends have told me that sometimes they feel like they don't even know me. This is because opening up fully has never been easy—it's something I constantly work on.

We learn to conceal our thoughts in the Church when we have viewpoints that are different from what is taught. For example, if I believe that the creation story is a metaphor while everyone in my men's group thinks it's literal, I will keep my opinions to myself to avoid rocking the boat and stirring up drama.

The opposite should be true with friendships outside the Church. Most guys don't care if you think differently from them—they're only looking for you to make a stance and have a solid reason for it. Your friend will respect you for that, even if he disagrees with you. This is true about everything from religious beliefs to your opinion on who will win the Super Bowl.

This is why male friendships outside the Church are a breath of fresh air. For the first time in your life, you are finally allowed to be your true self, which will open you up to some of the most rewarding friendships of your life.

The Optimal Structure of Your Social Life

What should your social life look like? How should it be structured?

Three aspects of a social life contribute to your happiness as a man:

- The people in your social life make you feel good.
- The people in your social life *do not* make you feel bad.

- The people in your social life teach you new things.

The first point is obvious. The second point is surprisingly less so as people often struggle to cut negative influences out of their lives, especially if they've known that person for a long time. I believe the third point is the key to really achieving a satisfying social life.

It's helpful to picture your social life like a target, in three concentric circles. Starting with the outermost circle and moving inward to the center (you), there are your acquaintances, your friends, and finally your inner circle.

Acquaintances are people you know but aren't friends with. These guys are decent enough, you make small talk when you see them, but other than that, your life and theirs don't intersect much. It's possible to have hundreds of acquaintances.

Your friends are guys you spend more time with. You know each other well. You do things together. You help each other out. When you deconverted, this layer of your social circle probably took the most damage.

Then there's the inner circle—the key to a fulfilling social life.

Guys in your inner circle are ones that you allow to influence you and change you for the better.

These guys have achieved something (usually advanced or complex) that you have envisioned for your own life and you want to learn from them how to get there. This could be any number of things: a successful business, a bodybuilder physique, or a healthy and long-term romantic relationship are just a few examples.

Your friends, by contrast, are great guys who you enjoy hanging out with, but you don't necessarily envision your life as resembling theirs.

Guys who become your friends usually do so after a period of time. Your inner circle should have no such time requirement. Most people (and especially men) consider their inner circle to be the guys they've been friends with the longest. This is not always best practice. Once you identify a man that you'd like to emulate and learn from, mentally slide him into your inner circle even if you've only known him for a day or two. Do what you can to increase the amount of time you spend talking to him or hanging out with him. Keep it within reason, though—don't annoy him.

Remember: You are the average of the five people you spend the most time with. Your goal is to structure your inner circle with that bit of wisdom in mind. The small group of people who get the most of your social time should consist of men who inspire you to become better, teach you new things, and correct you when you make a mistake.

Use the time you spend with your friends as a metric for how long you should spend interacting with someone in your inner circle. For example, if you spend two hours per week playing video games with your friends, then you should consider reducing that to one hour per week and dedicate the other hour to being in contact with someone from your inner circle.

Here's a sample social circle:

Acquaintances

- guys you know who are still in the Church
- guys you know from high school
- guys you see regularly at the bar you frequent

Friends

- guys you go out to eat with
- guys you watch sports with
- guys you relax with

Inner Circle

- a guy who's a world traveler
- a guy who's a competitive weightlifter
- an older ex-pastor who is further along in his deconversion journey than you

In this way, you can design your social life in a way that fulfills the various companionship needs you will have in a post-Church world.

Building a social life is a skill. Once learned, you can make precise goals for the kind of people you want in your inner circle, as friends, and those you keep as acquaintances.

How Large Should Your Social Life Be?

Is there a *quantity* of friends that is best? Is more always better? It could be that your social life gets too big and takes time away from other important life areas.

There are no clear parameters because each man will have different needs and different personalities and levels of introversion and extroversion. Therefore, all men will vary on how big of a social life they'll need to maintain happiness. So it's important that you determine what the best social structure *for you* looks like and then make a plan to build it.

You don't need to be, nor can you be, best friends with every guy you know. No one has time for that. As discussed before, when you grow older, your time for a social life decreases, which inversely increases the necessity of predominantly spending time with people who add to your life.

Big, bustling social lives can have pitfalls. They can be addicting. It's possible to know so many people that you get invites to events and parties every weekend. This a *good thing*, but if other areas of your life (such as your money or health) are suffering because of your expansive social calendar, you may need to lay down some boundaries. You may have to reallocate some of your time for other things you need to work on. You may need to practice saying "no."

Depending on how much of a social life you need to be happy, the guys you know outside your inner circle can be numerous, few, or even zero. The more relationships you have, the more you need to maintain. This could turn into a time suck, especially if these friends aren't adding value to your life or you aren't adding value to theirs.

Conclusion

A strong desire to spend time with male friends can sometimes be met with derision. You may feel (or be told) that your social life needs to fall behind other responsibilities such as your career and your family.

As I've tried to demonstrate here, your social life is an important piece of what makes you a happy and better man. After your deconversion, you may have to rebuild your social life from scratch. This takes time and hard work, but you should also view it as an opportunity to fill your life and inner circle with the high-quality men you were always meant to know.

You cannot live every possible type of life there is to live. You can't grow up both in the United States and Zimbabwe. You can't be both a CEO and a Hollywood actor. You can't be both a college professor and a sports star.

Each of our unique life paths lend themselves to diverse experiences and wisdom. It is always valuable to surround yourself with people who are different from you. Each person you meet may have a lesson to teach you that you may have never learned otherwise.

Chapter 9

YOUR HOBBIES

"The happiness of a man in this life does not consist in the absence but in the mastery of his passions." —Alfred Lord Tennyson

I am a writer.

Maybe that's obvious because of the book you are reading now. But before this book, I'd written many other things—fiction manuscripts, some screenplays, and half a musical I never finished. In fact, I've been a writer ever since I was very young. But before I was a writer, I was a drawer.

I don't remember when I first became obsessed with drawing. All kids draw, but then somewhere along the way they lose interest and quit. Not me. I wanted to get really good. I wanted to grow up and be a comic book artist.

So I drew. And drew and drew and drew. I never got better. Maybe that makes sense because I was a kid, but I also never got the right instruction. I never took a class.

The Deconverted Man

As I got older, I would use what little money I had to buy "How to draw" books and try to teach myself. But I never seemed to get better.

When I was in sixth grade, a locally famous caricature artist was hired by my middle school to teach a drawing class. I wanted to enroll, but his class was so popular that the school prioritized eighth graders (since it was their final year in junior high). I'd have to wait two years. In seventh grade I was forced to switch schools and lost my opportunity to take the class.

At that point, I committed to my other main hobby—writing.

The real reason I wanted to draw was so I could tell stories through pictures. If I sucked at drawing pictures, I could always tell the stories with words.

I especially loved the process of writing fiction. Anything I wanted to happen in a story I could make happen. Before, if I needed something to blow up, I had to figure out how to draw an explosion. That wasn't the case with writing stories. I could just describe the explosion.

There was just one problem, though. Despite the fact I was free to write about anything, I really *wasn't* free to write about anything. The plots, the thoughts and words of my characters, and even the themes of my stories had to align with what God found pleasing.

When I started college, I began to pursue writing professionally, focusing on younger, teenaged audiences. You may be familiar with the young adult category of books. It boasts such legends such as Harry Potter and *The Hunger Games*. I wanted to be one of those authors. But my work was stifled because I had to make sure that if, hypothetically, anyone from my church (or Jesus, for that matter) ever read it, it had to be "clean enough." And so my books always included a religious nod toward God, Jesus, or Christianity, always in a positive light.

You can probably imagine how hard it was to create a compelling villain who "wasn't allowed" to do truly terrible things in the story. Or characters who, when in intense life-or-death situations, never considered muttering a swear word. Or anti-hero protagonists who had to kill a few bad guys to save the day yet still be portrayed as the guy to root for. I'm sure if I went back and read those old manuscripts now, they would feel unrealistic and inauthentic.

All of this was compounded by the fact that my target audience was teenagers. I felt responsible for writing books that didn't contain objectionable content, as if I was the morality police dictating what they should read. At the same time, some young adult authors were putting out books with swearing, sex, violence, and other edgy content. I considered them in the wrong.

Later I read *On Writing*, Stephen King's famous memoir about the craft. One point in particular has always stuck with me: telling the truth.

If you've never read Stephen King, his books are packed with "objectionable content." His characters swear and blaspheme; they are racists, murders, rapists, occultists, and all the rest.

King said a minority of his haters would attribute those qualities to him as the author because he included them in his books. King maintained that the world is full of those kinds of people and that he wouldn't be telling the truth if he removed them from his stories or didn't represent them accurately. They did not represent *him*.

Intellectually I agreed, but I still couldn't break from my moral standpoint. I also wanted to tell the truth, but that truth would be Jesus.

One day, I felt fed up. I wanted to do something different. I wanted to write a story that featured all the stuff I was never allowed to write about before. I still don't know what snapped inside me, but I believe that every fundamentalist comes to a point where they just *have* to rebel, even in a small, insignificant way. So I wrote a novella with cursing, sex, and drinking. Almost all the characters were bad people. The plot was ridiculous. But I didn't care.

It was cathartic. I finished that story faster than any other I'd written. The words just flowed out of me as I got all that "bad" stuff off my chest and out of my system, stuff that had been building up for quite a while.

After I was done, I breathed a sigh of relief and tucked it somewhere in the depths of my hard drive, like the Ark of the Covenant at the end of *Raiders of the Lost Ark*. I'm sure if I read that story now, I'd laugh at the words of an innocent young man who thought he was being edgy but didn't really know the true meaning of the word.

After I wrote it, the world didn't end. God didn't punish me. My pastor never found out. And, most astoundingly, I didn't feel guilty. Not even the slightest bit. I felt that, for the first time, I had used my art to finally reflect the world around me—and inside me—which I had been trying to do since I'd stopped drawing.

It felt amazing.

What the Church Teaches You About Your Hobbies

"Use your gifts to glorify God."

We've all heard that sermon a time or two. And if you were like me, you probably took it to heart regarding your hobbies as well. That's why I felt like I couldn't "tell the truth" in my writing like Stephen King did.

- If you're a singer, maybe you felt you could only use your talents in the church's praise and worship band.
- If you're a filmmaker, maybe you felt you could only make Christian documentaries.
- If you're a painter, maybe you felt you could only paint scenes from Bible stories.

When you are only allowed to use your gifts to glorify God, your life is stifled.

Maybe you suppressed your interest in hobbies because the Church shamed you into "getting your priorities straight." The Church often positions itself as more important than our hobbies while proclaiming that glorifying God is more important than any "side interests." Your pastor might admonish you with, "You skipped Bible study on Wednesday night to study for your big exam, but you had time to play baseball with your friends on Saturday…"

He's got you there. You don't really have an argument for that one, because anything you say suggests that baseball is more important than God.

Depending on how much time you committed to the church and church functions, it's possible your hobbies fell by the wayside. Now that you've removed God from your worldview, it's the time to reconnect with the interests that made your life more colorful.

Make Your Hobbies a Part of Your Identity

This might be obvious to a lot of you but maybe it isn't to others who are introverted like me, so I think it's important to discuss. I'm talking about taking your hobbies another step by sharing them with others if you surpass the amateur level.

If you're a filmmaker, screen your latest film publicly or enter it into film festivals.

If you're a singer, take your vocal cords from the shower to a live audience or make some recordings.

If you're a painter, have an exhibition to show off your skills and artistic vision.

Also, notice that I said, "If you're a filmmaker." I didn't say, "If you like to make films." Own your talent and interest by boldly applying the term to yourself.

At first, I didn't do this with my writing. Whenever I told people about my attempts to get published, it would ultimately lead to a barrage of questions. I'd try to downplay my efforts by saying something lame like, "Yeah, I like to write sometimes."

Don't do what I did. Own it. These days I say, "Yes, I'm a writer."

The High-Concept Hook

A high-concept hook is a term often used in the film industry. If your idea for a movie can be described succinctly and effectively in one sentence (also known as a log line or an elevator pitch), then you have a high-concept hook. This is valuable in Hollywood. Movies with high-concept hooks have a higher chance of getting made and watched than those that do not.

You can extend this concept to yourself. Whenever you meet new people, you inevitably get the same, boring, small-talk questions. "What do you do?" Perhaps you, too, are guilty of uttering these words at a party. People usually declare their profession.

"I'm a chemical engineer."

"I'm a teacher."

"I'm a lawyer."

"Oh," the other person says, nodding politely. "That's cool."

This is essentially the elevator pitch of yourself, the one-line "hook" that piques interest—or not. However, when you proudly claim your hobbies as part of your identity, you set yourself apart from the masses. You are automatically more interesting. You now have a high-concept hook.

"I'm a chemical engineer but I'm also a DJ."

"I'm a teacher but also a sculptor."

"I'm a lawyer but also an equestrian."

"Oh, wow," they say, eyebrows rising in interest. "Tell me more."

Better yet, if you have improved beyond the amateur level of your hobby, show them pictures of your artwork on your cell phone and then invite them to your next exhibition. Let them listen to a song you recorded, then invite them to your next performance. Play a video of your latest martial arts match, then invite them to watch you compete.

The meek do not inherent the earth—they bore the earth. The earth is inherited by people who put a valuable piece of themselves into the world.

Hobbies and Your Happiness

We all know a guy who doesn't really do anything and isn't involved in anything. He could be super nice and cool, but we can't help but feel that he's a bit dull. Maybe I'm describing you.

Doing stuff makes most people happy. This is doubly true for men. Give a man a task, no matter how meaningless or arbitrary, and watch him instantly transform. A Rubik's Cube, a jigsaw puzzle, or a leaky pipe. Watch his brow furrow and his eyes squint as his brain works to figure out how to accomplish the job set in front of him.

To the male brain, this is a task that needs to be completed and nothing else will get its attention until the job is done. This is the blessing of being a man. We find pleasure in accomplishing things. Give yourself something to do and you'll be happier than when you were idling on the couch.

If you're ever feeling down, or in a funk, or going through a stressful situation, your hobbies are there to take your mind off the negativity. It's a healthy outlet for refocusing on something positive rather than indulging in something negative such as drugs or alcohol.

When you felt this way before deconversion, you probably prayed. You asked God to change your mood or temperament. As discussed before, this is the same as inactivity. It's passive and lazy. Your hobbies provide just the opposite. They are enjoyable and challenging; they engage your brain and will lift your spirits during these down times.

Reserve Time for Your Hobbies

Time. That's always the excuse, isn't it? We never seem to have enough amidst all of our other responsibilities. When you're laden with careers, families, and kids, it can be hard to justify spending time in the garage working on your motorcycle or building model airplanes.

Like your social life, your hobbies are often the first to get booted at the first sign of busyness.

Defend against this as best you can. Remember, you are reading this book to take back control of your life. You've resolved to no longer be swept up in the riptide.

Get creative. Budget your time with a schedule. Combine life areas—maybe your social time spent with the guys doubles as your hobby time, like getting together for a poker night.

Participating in your hobby once a week can often be sufficient. In fact, if you overindulge the time spent on your hobbies, it can become a distraction, which could negatively impact your health, money, or family.

What If You Have No Hobbies?

Are you like the hypothetical guy I described earlier who's not really involved in anything? Or maybe you committed all your free time to the Church and never invested the effort to learn what interests *you* instead of what interests God.

Embrace your curiosity. What have you always wanted to learn? Or try? Or do? If you live in even a medium-sized city, you can easily find out where those things are happening.

Step out of your comfort zone and give it a shot.

Have you read the previous section and started implementing the steps described to improve and expand your social life? This is often the easiest introduction to new hobbies. What are your friends interested in? What do they do for fun? Ask if you can accompany them.

This method also works if you want to add new hobbies to the list of activities you already enjoy.

Monetizing Your Hobbies

If you practice your hobby enough to where you've improved beyond the amateur level, it's possible that you can start getting paid for it.

Singers, you can be hired to perform at events, such as weddings.

Painters, you can sell your artwork.

Woodworkers, you can build furniture for clients.

Or you can be paid to teach others how to do these things. Perhaps you're already an expert in a hobby you've had for your entire life. That's even better. Have you considered monetizing it? If not, get on it!

Supplementing your income while also engaging in a healthy, productive hobby improves your financial standing as we discussed in the section about your money. The simplest, easiest, or quickest additional income source you can add to your life is most often a monetized hobby.

Are you beginning to see where all the dots connect? The different areas of your life really do start to complement each other when you finally remove God from the equation.

"Dangerous" Hobbies

Ideally, your hobbies should add to you as a person. They should enrich you and encourage you to grow and develop. And sometimes, they may even earn you money on the side.

However, there are some hobbies I consider "dangerous" because they can become addicting and huge time sucks. I'm *not* saying these hobbies are bad. If they bring you enjoyment, great, but I would encourage you to set a timer when engaging in them.

I personally have gotten lost in each of the hobbies on this list, so I know just how many valuable hours can be lost if you aren't closely monitoring your time doing them.

Video Games

If you excessively play MMORPGs, online shooters, single player campaigns, or addicting cell phone games, it may be time to consider some more productive uses of your time.

Think about it. These games usually involve controlling a make-believe character, leveling them up, going through trials and triumphs, and experiencing an interesting story. What if you could do all of this for yourself in real life?

I'm not saying you should never play video games. I understand they can be relaxing, and I do enjoy playing every now and then when I find a game I really like. However, I *am* suggesting that you put a limit on the amount of time you spend playing per week, especially if you have work to do in other areas of your life, such as your health and your money. Remember, it's all about balance.

Watching Sports

I can relate hard to this one. After a long week at school, it felt great to just sit on the couch on Saturday and watch six straight hours of college football. It was easy to binge because the next game started as soon as the current one finished.

It took me a while to realize how much time I was sinking into an activity that wasn't improving my life but merely distracting me from it.

Again, like video games, I'm not telling you to stop watching sports completely. You can still follow your favorite team and watch their games. But you don't need to watch *every* televised college football or NFL game. When you watch sports, you are seeing athletes who have dedicated thousands of hours to their practice, testing their skills against opposing forces and overcoming trials and tribulations. Our male brains connect strongly with these things.

Can you find those actions and emotions within your own story? Not so easily, but that doesn't mean you don't have your own heroic journey waiting for you to embrace it. You've already deconverted; that's a huge first step.

Internet Surfing

This one ensnares me more than the previous two items combined.

We're all familiar with the internet rabbit hole. You hop onto your browser to look up something, and before you know it, you have forty-seven tabs open and you're reading entire Wikipedia articles.

In my case, I rationalized this is as "learning" so it wasn't *too* bad, right? Well, it is when what I'm "learning" has no direct application to my immediate life.

YouTube and social media sites are *designed* to be like this, by the way. The algorithms that run these sites track your interests and puts that content directly in front of your eyeballs to keep you hooked. They even purposely present you with inflammatory, controversial, or click-bait content because they know your primal brain can't resist the temptation.

Resist anyway. Take back control of your brain and attention. Don't overstimulate yourself with hits of dopamine. Put a firm time limit on your internet surfing and then close your device.

Conclusion

It can be tempting to minimize hobbies in the process of getting your life together. The rewards aren't always as obvious as when sorting out other things such as your money or your health. But I implore you not to forget this area of your life.

What you do determines who you are. You can no longer fall back on the stock cliché of embracing your "identity in Christ." No one can even explain what that means. You are now free to build your own identity; you can do and be whatever you want. The things you do for fun, for enrichment, and to relax are equally valuable parts of who you are as a person.

Never forget that.

Chapter 10

YOUR RELATIONSHIPS WITH WOMEN

> *"If so many men, so many minds, certainly so many hearts, so many kinds of love."* —Leo Tolstoy

I stood in my first wedding when I was 21 years old.

A good friend of mine was getting married. Both the bride and the groom were the same age as me. The entire church congregation had been invited and were overjoyed by the union. This couple had long been held up by the church as an ideal example of a godly dating scenario.

From what I can remember, it was a fine ceremony. But what I remember most vividly about that day wasn't the ceremony or the couple but what I was feeling: utterly unprepared to be a husband. I know now that it was normal for me to feel that way because I was only 21, but I honestly thought there was something wrong with me, that I was immature and not developing as a normal adult. After all, marriage is God's ultimate desire for the people in his Church. Who was I to reject that? All my life

I'd been told that 21 was plenty old enough to enter into a lifetime commitment with another human. But I wasn't feeling it.

What the Church Teaches You About Relationships with Women

The Church's teachings and doctrines on this subject could possibly be the worst, most damaging thing they teach.

When the topic of sex, dating, and relationships within the Church comes up, the discussion is mostly centered around "purity culture." Purity culture was a movement in evangelical churches during the 1990s and early 2000s that pushed a shame-based paradigm of dating, relationships, and sexual abstinence, most often targeted at the Church's young women. Many adult women who were subjected to these teachings when they were teenagers report lingering hang ups and trauma regarding sex, their bodies, and how they conduct themselves in romantic relationships.

Since purity culture mostly affected women, men are often left out of the discussion. The truth is that the Church's teachings aimed at men in regards to sex, relationships, abstinence, and traditional gender roles are also very damaging and need to be sorted through.

In the Church, men repeatedly hear the same message about the sanctity of marriage. We are slowly "groomed for marriage" and constantly told how, in the future, we will be the spiritual leader of our household. Having a wife and kids is held up as the ideal, the goal to strive for, and an ultimate blessing from God.

Let me be clear—those things are *not bad*. However, the Church generally has *no regard* for age or life situation when encouraging a man to marry his girlfriend. In fact, when a man tells his pastor, peers, or men's group that he's thinking about marriage, they automatically talk about God's plan, God's timing, and how she's "the one." The decision to marry is overwhelmingly praised by the entire church body because they see this as God's great design.

The Church generally deems a young man ready to marry if he is "strong in his faith." They believe a strong faith is all he needs to navigate the maelstrom he's inviting into his life. Any husband-to-be who expresses concern about his life situation (a lack of an education or financial resources or the inexperience of youth, as just a few examples) is overwhelmed by a mountain of (ultimately damaging) reassurances by older church members:

- "There is never a right time!"
- "Beth and I were nineteen when we got married and had nothing. It was challenging, but we made it work!"
- "Just trust in God. You two will figure it out!"

What you end up with is an emotionally charged engagement and wedding marked by dangerously little logic or strategic life planning. But the couple doesn't care about that; they only care that their friends get to dress up, have a party, dance, praise Jesus, celebrate God's plan, and make stupid "wedding night" jokes. After the honeymoon is over, you end up with two young, inexperienced, unsettled, and unstable people trying to rapidly grow into a life that doesn't fit them yet.

The Church has no qualms about encouraging people to get married who are too young, too immature, too inexperienced, too naive, or too emotionally unprepared because they think that is what God wants.

Why Men in the Church Get Married Too Young

There are numerous reasons this happens, and none of them are good:

- By their early to mid-twenties, most Christian men have realized that they aren't going to overcome their lust or beat their sexual sin, so they figure they can marry their girlfriend and, like flipping a switch, make their sexuality approved of by God.
- Some Christian men are pressured by their girlfriend to get married. Her friends are all getting married and she doesn't want to be last, so she pushes him to propose.
- A Christian man can also feel pressure from his pastor or men's group. If he's been dating his girlfriend for five or six years, that's often considered way too long. He needs to "man up" and make a real commitment.
- Although rarely explicitly stated, there is a strong social stigma against being an "older" unmarried member of the church. I put "older" in quotes because the age at which this occurs isn't old at all. Still single at the age of thirty and

people will start to wonder. They will ask when you plan on settling down or offer to set you up with someone. In extreme cases, they begin to wonder if you even like women.

I'm aware that some of these situations also occur outside of the Church. However, I found the listed scenarios to be alarmingly prevalent within the Church.

Removing God from Your Relationships with Women

This may prove to be one of the biggest deconversion projects you will undertake. It's not just a simple mindset change. If you were in the Church long enough, you may have deeply rooted beliefs that you need to excise. You may even have deep trauma. Unfortunately, the shaming of natural sexual desires, homophobia, and sexual abuse are rampant within the Church. Getting over that can be an uphill battle.

This topic could fill an entire volume on its own. For now, I will speak separately to single guys and married guys. Each will have a subsection dedicated to helping you navigate a world where God has been removed from your relationships with women.

Single Guys

First, a clarification: If you have a girlfriend you aren't married to, you are single.

Before you start dating, you need to *unlearn* everything the Church taught you regarding relationships with women. None of it will help you going forward.

Relationships with women can be fun and rewarding but they can also be disastrous. Handling them incorrectly can have serious repercussions on both your life and hers.

Don't Have Serious Relationships Until You're Older

Before we start, resolve right now to not have any serious relationships until you have addressed *all* of the other life areas described in this book. I define a serious relationship as any or a combination of the following items:

- legal marriage
- living with a woman in a romantic or domestic context
- promising a woman you'll be her romantic partner forever
- having children with a woman

Invest in yourself *first* before adding the responsibility of a long-term romantic partner into your life.

I'm serious. Do it now. Make a solemn vow to yourself.

Arnold Schwarzenegger said in his biography that accomplishing one's major life goals should come before long-term relationships and kids and he's right.[1] Arnold is one of the greatest men who has ever lived, and when a man like him speaks, you shut up and listen!

Before incorporating a woman or partner into your life, you need to become the man you want to be. Get your money, investments, career, and health in order before getting serious with someone. It also helps to have had plenty of meaningful life experiences. That's why this section comes after all the others.

One of the most advantageous things about being a man is that you can have kids at almost any age. Most men forfeit this advantage because of one specific woman they think is "the one," and because of her "biological clock," she will pressure the man to marry her and have kids with her. Most men give in.

Men who have kids too young severely restrict themselves. With a family, it's much harder to take risks, build a business, travel, maintain health, hang out with friends, or enjoy hobbies. Not impossible, but much harder.

A basic, blanket rule I would give to all young men is to resist having a serious girlfriend or relationship until age 35. Forty is even better.

If you beg to differ on this advice, bear with me and read on.

"The One" Does not Exist

When you take God out of the equation, you are forced to admit that "the one" does not exist in the common, Church-approved meaning. And it's a ridiculous concept to begin with. Most people marry someone from their same university or town or church. You mean to tell me that out of the 3.5 billion women on this planet, "the one" happened to be a member of your local church?

When you confront the fact that God does not exist and therefore no one has a master plan for your future wife and marriage, you begin to understand that your relationships with women are completely under your control. There is no longer any pressure from fundamentalists to rush into anything. There is no "God's plan."

If you are 21 years old and dating a woman you love, understand that this isn't the only woman in your entire life you could ever possibly love. Likewise, you aren't the only man that she could ever love. Both of you will meet other people who would potentially make great partners.

Therefore, there is never any reason to "lock down" a particular woman or relationship. If you both love each other and she wants to get married but you aren't ready, rest assured it will be safe to let her go to a man who *is* ready. You two were not designed as a couple by God before you both were born. There is another man right around the corner who can marry this girl and give her a good life and family. There is also another woman right around the corner who will make you very happy. You aren't losing "the one" or messing up God's plan by listening to your gut and choosing yourself.

It's okay to love someone while knowing, even at the very genesis of the relationship, that it won't last forever.

Relearning How to Date

Now that you've agreed to wait until *at least* age 35 before you have a serious, long-term relationship, committed to becoming the ideal version of yourself first, and understand that there is no such thing as "the one," where do you go from here? You will still meet plenty of cool women as you go through life, and you'll want to date them even though you're refraining from anything serious or long-term.

As you conduct your relationships with women post-deconversion, you'll be doing a lot of things differently. You won't, for example, be attending your church's singles functions and wait to be introduced to a friend of a friend and then call it God's divine plan. You will be entering relationships with deconverted women or women that were non-believers all along and the rules will change.

But first you need to unlearn what you were taught in church.

The Problem with Pursuit

In your Church days, you were probably told to "pursue" a woman or to "pursue" her heart. The ladies, in their Bible studies, were told to wait for a man who was willing to "pursue" them. All the popular Christian books by trendy pastors reiterated this point over and over.

The precise meaning of a properly executed pursuit varies from person to person, but the basic gist was that the man is expected to do most, if not all, of the following things:

- take the woman out on countless dinner dates and pay for all of them.
- plan fun and creative dates like horseback riding, rock climbing, or day trips and, again, pay for all of them.
- give thoughtful gifts.
- spend lots of time "being approved of" by the girl's friends.
- expect the bare minimum of physical intimacy, which could mean as little as a one-armed side

hug. If the girl wanted to do more, it was the man's job to put a stop to it.

Through it all, the ultimate goal of marriage loomed heavy in the back of the couple's mind—a twenty-ton ball of pressure that isn't good for any budding relationship. And even with all this time, money, and effort spent upfront by the man, the girl is under no obligation to return the affection or agree to any relationship.

How many of you, despite months of effort similar to the list above, were eventually served one of these lines:

- "You're like a brother to me."
- "I feel like God is telling me this isn't the right relationship for me."
- "I just want to be in a relationship with Jesus right now."

What a waste of time. Thankfully, now that you've deconverted, all that crap about pursuit goes right out the window.

Dating Outside the Church

In general, women in the Church sit patiently in the pews, praying and waiting for their spiritual husband to scoop them up and carry them away to a romanticized, Instagram-worthy Christian marriage. Women outside the Church would be offended if they were told to behave like that.

The modern woman is independent, has goals, makes her own money, and wants to build her own ideal life before getting serious with a man. Being pursued by a man she isn't interested in wastes her time and annoys her.

When you approach a woman that you are attracted to (in person, via text, through a dating app, etc.), you should be able to tell reasonably quickly if she's interested in you. If she isn't, don't be like the guys in the Church and start "pursuing." Pursuing means you're assuming she's wrong to reject you and that you can convince her otherwise. That's rude, presumptuous, and frankly a bit pathetic. In the *real* dating world outside the Church, pursuit is one small step away from harassment.

Instead, you move on. A girl around the corner *will* be interested in you.

The Iron Law

How do you tell if a girl is interested in you? Easy. If she makes an effort to spend time with you in a dating or romantic context, she's interested. This leads to the Iron Law that you should always keep in mind when dating:

If a woman wants to spend time with you, she will always find a way to make it happen.

It doesn't matter how busy she is. She will skip class, leave work early, go to work late, cancel on her friends, or skip a workout to make time to be with you. When you keep this law in mind, you can quickly determine your chances of success. If you keep getting the runaround, then she isn't interested enough. If she insists that she *is* interested but all other activities in her life are taking precedence, then respect how committed she is to the many facets of her life and accept that the timing is wrong. Stop trying and move on.

Only Attempt to Meet Up with Her Twice

Most women are bad at telling you directly that they aren't interested in dating you. They don't want to hurt your feelings. As men, this is annoying because we'd rather just know so we can move on. But this is the way life is and you just have to accept it.

Fortunately, the Iron Law is there to help you work around this. To test it, I suggest making only two attempts to connect with a woman you are interested in. More than that and you risk wasting your time and annoying her.

If you call her and she says she'd like to meet up but can't because she's busy and doesn't offer an alternative time, graciously say you understand, no worries. After a week, try again. If you get the same answer, she simply isn't interested enough. Time to move on. She'll be relieved that you get it and that she doesn't have to hurt your feelings by being more direct. This is the direct opposite of the pursuit model practiced in the Church.

You Shouldn't Have to Try too Hard

When two people are attracted to each other, the process of connecting should be relatively seamless and smooth. If it's not, then the attraction isn't strong enough or the timing might be off. It shouldn't be too difficult.

If you feel like you are constantly trying to convince

women to give you a shot or working too hard to impress or attract them, then something is wrong. That something is probably you. You need to immediately stop and take a look inward. Almost always, the reason you are trying so hard is because you are not yet the kind of man that women want to date.

I did not say that you are *not* the kind of man women want to date. I said you are *not yet* the man that women want to date. There is a very strong difference.

Why do you have to *become* that man? Why can't you just *be* that man?

Because our caveman ancestors played by different rules. Women were valued for their beauty and ability to have babies. Men were valued for their abilities to hunt, build, fight, and protect. This means women can just be. Men must *become*.

A man doesn't magically grow into having the skills that make him valuable as a woman naturally grows into her beauty and ability to bear children. A man must learn these skills, usually from a tribe of older, more experienced men.

We no longer live like tribal cavemen today, but our bodies and brains evolve more slowly than the society and technology around us. Therefore, the basic premise still applies—at some point in his life, a man must still *become* a man.

If you've recently deconverted, there's a high possibility that you need to "become" again and grow into the man you truly are instead of the man who constantly conformed to please God.

And what kind of men do women like to date?

- A man who can make enough money to be secure and take care of his loved ones.
- A man who is disciplined enough to improve and maintain his health.
- A man who has a healthy relationship with his family.
- A man who has a strong and wide social network of other men.
- A man who is engaged in at least one interesting hobby.
- A man who knows how to handle his relationships with women by exhibiting emotional control, stability, leadership, and maturity.

Does any of that sound familiar? It should. Developing those qualities *prior to pursuing a serious relationship* has been the focus of the previous sections. Once implemented, you will have become the kind of man that women want to date and it will be that much easier to attract them.

How to Conduct Your Relationship

Once you've met a cool girl who you'd like to have a relationship with, then great! How you conduct your relationship with her is entirely up to you and her.

Your pastor cannot tell you what your relationship needs to look like. Older married couples cannot tell you anything either. Your men's group also gets no say.

Perhaps for the first time in your life, what your relationships look like is entirely up to you. This means your relationship can fall anywhere between casual sex once a week to something deep and loving.

The idea of a relationship that is nothing more than casual sex may be hard for recently deconverted men to get on board with. The Church would be aghast at anyone conducting their relationship in such a manner. But the Church wrongly believes it has the authority to tell two consenting adults how to behave and what to do with their bodies. You may have also witnessed men in these kinds of relationships being shamed and told they were sinful, dirty, or perhaps even abusive.

The truth is that women outside of the Church are just as willing to have a purely sexual relationship as men are. They have other things going on in their lives—career, interests, travel—and may be just as resolved as you to wait until they are older before beginning a serious, long-term relationship.

Here are a couple of things to keep in mind:

Don't overinvest into or overidealize the relationship.

Even if you really like each other (or love each other) there is no such thing as "the one" and God's plan did not bring you two together. Even if you love her, never forget that there are many other women out there that you could potentially love. Conversely, there are many other men besides you that your partner could also build a loving relationship with.

Don't let the relationship replace other areas of your life.

Younger men are particularly susceptible to this, especially if they haven't had a lot of relationship experience yet. As you become closer to this special lady, there's a tendency for the two of you to start spending more time together. This feels good, but if this happens, you need to recognize it as quickly as possible.

If your relationship starts to consume more and more of your time, then you will have less time for the other areas of your life that keep you happy. A man's social life, hobbies, and health are the areas that usually get damaged when they dedicate too much time to their relationship. As I demonstrated earlier in the book, being out of balance will make you unhappy, even if it seems like spending more time with your partner is making you happy *for now*.

Have a plan for when the relationship changes.

If your partner breaks up with you, it's normal to feel sad or a little disappointed. But if you've followed the other advice I've laid out in this chapter (and the entire book) then there should be no reason to have an emotional breakdown, be depressed, or mope around for weeks. She was not "the one" and never was. There is someone else who will make you just as happy (probably happier) right around the corner. If you feel like you need time to be single for a while, awesome! Invest your time into other areas of your life that will bring you happiness (such as your social life, hobbies, and health) until you feel ready to date again.

On the other hand, if you have already spent considerable time investing in yourself by following the advice laid out in this book, then the relationship is more likely to change in the opposite way—she'll want to get more serious.

As a reminder, I define a serious, long-term relationship as:

- legal marriage
- living with a woman in a romantic or domestic context
- promising a woman you'll be her romantic partner forever
- having children with a woman

When you were in the Church, you were always taught that a serious, long-term relationship was the ultimate goal. You and your girlfriend enthusiastically rushed toward this specific finish line because you were taught that this was God's ultimate desire.

Now that you recognize this as false, you are better prepared to make a mature, informed decision about your relationship. Getting into a serious, long-term relationship will greatly decrease the amount of time you can spend building your ideal life. If you don't believe me, ask any older married man, especially one that has kids.

If you are under the age of 35 or if you can honestly say you have more work to do on yourself, then you need to uphold your boundary and honestly explain to your girlfriend that you are not ready for the kind of relationship that she wants and that you want to keep things the way they are.

If she agrees, great. If not, then you need to let her go. She's told you that she's ready for a serious, long-term relationship and since she is not "the one" then you need to allow her to find another man who is ready to give her that kind of relationship.

I understand this approach may come off as pessimistic or distrustful toward relationships in general. However, if you've recently deconverted and are actively rebuilding your life post-fundamentalism, I would prefer your walls to be up rather than down and for you to be very discerning.

In general, men have a tendency to believe that a new relationship will be a long-term answer to their problems, either directly or indirectly. It isn't. A new relationship will be fun and make you feel good for a little while (the honeymoon phase usually lasts about three months) but then as familiarity sets in, the realities of the relationship will emerge—that it involves work, time, money, and emotional energy, among many other things.

It is just so much simpler—and far more effective—to work on yourself when you don't have the responsibility of a partner tossed into the mix.

You should never believe that a new relationship is the answer to any problem you might have. A new relationship is meant to be a complement to your life, not something you use to distract yourself from pain or responsibility. And frankly, since women are highly intuitive, she'll figure it out pretty quickly if this is your reason for being in a relationship with her.

Sex and Shame

It's very likely that even though you've deconverted, you still have hang-ups and shame related to sexuality. Sexual shame is usually associated with women in the Church and with good reason: They've been routinely judged for their bodies, clothes, and behaviors.

However, sexual shame affects men in the Church as well. Pastors around the globe regularly condemn men's natural desires—physical attraction toward women, an urge to masturbate, or stealing peeks at pornography, to name a few. This may have led you to exert great effort and energy trying to beat that sin by removing sexual thoughts, "bouncing your eyes," and confessing to your mentors when you slipped up and visited a dirty website.

Such suppression can damage your psyche. If it goes on long enough, you can potentially erode your natural sexuality by suppressing the very real desires you feel in your gut and heart, making it very difficult to have normal relationships. This can manifest in many negative ways:

- You end up undereducated about sex and sexuality.
- You feel shameful and dirty after having sex with your partner.
- You can't perform sexually because of erectile dysfunction or because of disinterest in sex altogether.

Getting over the shame and guilt can be a long process for some men. Speak with a therapist if you feel you aren't making meaningful progress.

Your Sexuality

Humans are sexual creatures. Like, very sexual.

A person's sexuality is comparable to an iceberg—a small obvious bit above a large and wide expanse hidden below the surface. Most fundamentalists only experience the tip and suppress the rest that lurks beneath the surface because they consider it sinful. That's another reason for the deconverted man to wait a few years before settling into a long-term relationship: You need to figure out what you like sexually.

While in the Church, you likely suppressed your sexuality and convinced yourself that you were only allowed to like one type of girl—a good, old fashioned Church girl. But that is rarely true. The submerged part of most everyone's sexual iceberg contains all the stuff that isn't talked about in Church—fantasies, desires, preferences, and even fetishes.

You should now feel welcome and empowered to explore these areas beneath the surface, have some experiences, and learn who you are as a sexual being. I've heard it said before that you never truly know yourself until you understand the full depths of your sexuality. This is a Pandora's box worth opening. The possibilities of what you might find are endless:

- Maybe you prefer women of a certain ethnicity.
- Maybe you like women with lots of tattoos.
- Maybe you like dominant women.
- Maybe you prefer bisexual women.
- Maybe you yourself are bisexual.
- Maybe you are looking for a swinger lifestyle.

- You might discover that you're polyamorous.
- You might discover that you like to conduct your relationships non-monogamously so that both you and your partner have the freedom to explore.

When you are no longer restricted to the "good and godly woman" archetype, you are free to experiment with a myriad of options and possibilities. Nothing will make you unhappier than discovering you have a certain preference or fantasy but got married at age 23 to a church girl who isn't on board.

Female Sexuality

If you've spent significant time in the Church, then it's possible you've internalized a myriad of myths regarding female sexuality.

The Church teaches an entirely incorrect narrative of women and sex because it wants to control female sexuality. They do this with practices such as purity culture, virginity pledges, and encouraging courting over dating. The reasons the Church seeks to control female sexuality are numerous, but I think it essentially boils down to them being threatened by it. If women in the Church had more autonomous control over their bodies and sexuality, then it would weaken the male-dominant hierarchy that most churches have. Even more tragic is that most female congregation members believe these falsehoods more often than not.

Here are a few truths regarding female sexuality that

the Church knows but refuses to acknowledge and attempts to suppress:

- Women crave sex just as much, if not more, than men.
- Women masturbate just as much, if not more, than men.
- Women consume pornography just as much, if not more, than men.
- Women want to experience multiple sexual partners just as much, if not more, than men.
- Women have numerous sexual fantasies and I'm sure a lot of them would make most men blush.

I could go on.

It's in your best interest to be honest with yourself (and your female partner) about female sexuality because most men within the Church never are. They have an incorrect view of their girlfriends and wives because they prefer to remain ignorant about their partner's true desires. Instead of saying, "Your desires are weird and wrong in the eyes of God, so stop tempting me," the deconverted man willingly satisfies his partner's sexual needs and desires.

Practice Safe Sex

With all that being said, I need to remind you to *always* practice safe sex. The safest way to have sex (besides abstinence) is to wear a condom every single time you have sex, no matter what, even if you've been dating someone for a long time. As I discussed in Chapter 6, condoms are the safest form of contraception regarding a man's sexual health.

To briefly reiterate (because it's that important), condoms are superior because they are the only form of birth control you can *control*. You can't *control* your partner forgetting to take her birth control pill or if her IUD malfunctions. Also, female birth control does not protect against sexually transmitted diseases.

In extreme cases, you can't be sure that a new partner is telling you the truth about her birth control practices. That's a grim thing to think about, but it does happen and more often than you may think. The last thing you want is an unexpected pregnancy with a woman you didn't expect to spend your life with. There is simply too much at stake to be careless about your contraception.

Married Guys

Things get trickier if you married a Christian girl when you were a Christian. The relationship has likely lasted longer, you've combined money and assets, and there are probably some kids in the picture. If this marriage were to end, a lot more is at stake.

First, a word of encouragement. You aren't wrong, bad, or evil for deconverting. You can't help what you believe or feel, and your new truth is as much a part of you as your personality. It is nothing to be ashamed of.

That said, this situation can still be very challenging. In your believing spouse's mind, she signed up for a Christian marriage and a Christian family and now you are changing the contract. She has a right to feel this way so be empathetic as you navigate these waters.

When deconverting as a married Christian, you essentially have three potential outcomes:

1. You and your spouse stay together and she continues to believe while you do not.
2. You and your spouse stay together and she eventually deconverts with you.
3. You and your spouse divorce.

You may prefer Option #2, but you have to remember that you cannot control anyone—not even your wife. Like you, she's an adult and has the autonomy to experience her own emotions and make her own decisions for how to deal with this and go forward. Therefore, your goal during this time is to

- avoid arguments, fights, and drama
- resist trying to deconvert her by reciting facts and logic
- be patient
- be strong

Keeping all this in mind, there is no finger-snap solution to resolving the situation, but here are some ideas to make the transition smoother. And it won't happen overnight. It may take a year or more to bring things back into balance.

Step 1: Declare Your New Beliefs Once

As you did with your family, you need to make it clear what you now believe and do not believe. And don't make the declaration without careful thought. You need to be clear about where you are in your deconversion because you will be owning it for a long time.

As discussed in the section about telling your family about your deconversion, you can use similar tactics with your wife. Write down everything and practice telling her in the mirror or give her a letter and be sure you are present and available to discuss it.

Decide what you are and are not willing to do. Will you still be attending church on Sunday? Will you continue to lead the family in prayer before dinner? Will you read Bible stories with your children? Decide and then stick to it. Don't skip something one week and do it the next. That will just confuse your wife (and kids) and give her hope that you're coming back.

You don't necessarily need to abstain from everything you used to do. You might need to make some concessions, especially if there are young children involved. It's up to you and your specific family situation.

Remember, the goal is to avoid useless arguments and drama. If you need to say a twenty second prayer in front of your in-laws every now and then to avoid an argument, just do it.

All of this should be declared only once. It will likely be an emotional discussion, so after it's done, there is no need for you to bring it up over and over again.

Step 2: Shut Up

Once you've declared your new stance, you need to shut up about it.

I know this is challenging for newly deconverted men.

There is a strong desire to talk about all your new knowledge and deconstruct your past to get through the trauma of having believed a lie for so long. Fine, but your still-believing wife is *not* the person to do it with—at least not yet. There are countless internet forums and social media groups that offer a much better outlet for this.

Also, clean up your evidence. Don't leave that Richard Dawkins book on your reading table or Christopher Hitchens videos in your YouTube search history. While these things might seem negligible to you, your wife my interpret them as subtle attacks on her beliefs.

Be strong and patient when your wife brings up your deconversion. If she isn't asking for new information or to better understand your point of view, she is probably looking for a fight. Don't engage. Find a way to end the conversation as quickly as possible. If you argue, it will confirm her bias that non-Christians are evil and want to attack the faithful. You are not like that.

And of course, don't try to deconvert her or convince her. Remember all the times when you still believed and nonbelievers tried to talk you out of your faith? Your guard was up and your mind was closed. The same applies to her.

Step 3: Become a Better Man

Use the preceding sections of this book to build an ideal, post-fundamentalist version of yourself. Don't announce what you're doing. Talk doesn't matter—only action does. So just start doing.

Brainstorm some ideas for additional income sources and then build them. Get on a workout and diet program.

Pick up a new hobby and meet some cool guy friends along the way.

Be a better husband than you were before. Be nice. Be empathetic. But remain firm in your new certainties.

After a period of time, you'll be a better man than you were when you believed. You'll be wealthier, healthier, and happier. Your wife will notice. In time, she'll come to like and respect the deconverted version of you more than the one God was in charge of making.

Step 4: Determine which Outcome Is Most Likely

As time goes on and you execute this plan successfully, you'll start to get a feel for the future of your marriage. Perhaps your wife is inspired by your growth, and now that the initial shock of your deconversion has passed, is willing to listen to your thoughts, especially because you didn't try to push your beliefs onto her.

If your spouse deconverts with you, then great! That will be a grand new adventure for you both. Maybe you can gently proceed uncovering your icebergs together.

Maybe your wife shows no signs of deconversion but is becoming accustomed to having a separate-faith marriage. Maybe she'll realize that keeping you as a life partner is more important than her childhood dream of being in a Church family.

These outcomes are ideal. But what if she never seems to accept your change? What do you do if your marriage continues to be strained by your deconversion? If that looks like the case, it might be time for you and your wife to go your separate ways.

Relationships are about the happiness of the two

people involved, not about ensuring arbitrary longevity at any cost. If neither of you are happy being in a mixed-faith marriage, look for an opportunity to make her an offer. For example, if she makes a rude, passive-aggressive remark about atheists or your deconversion, say something like this:

"We've been trying this for a while now and you still seem quite unhappy with my change. Do you think it would be best if we went our separate ways?"

When you say it, be thoughtful and earnest. Ask it as a genuine question that shows your concern for her. If she gets flabbergasted and acts surprised, then nod, end the conversation, and leave. She probably won't bring it up again. She'll understand that her negativity about your deconversion triggered your offer and might convince her to resist making similar comments in the future. If that's the case, you may have just saved your marriage.

If she agrees, then you can proceed from there. Even if you don't want your marriage to end, you won't be truly happy being married to a woman who doesn't want to be married to you.

The Goal of a Relationship is Happiness, Not Longevity

This concept might take a little while to sink in because the Church, and even society outside of the Church, teaches this ass backwards.

I'm sure you've experienced this in your men's group or on a men's retreat. The church finds the oldest man they can and has him speak on marriage and relationships. He begins by qualifying, "I've been married to my wife for forty-five years..." All the ears in the room perk up. All eyes go to him. Everyone sits up straight and gives him their undivided attention.

Wow, everyone thinks to themselves. *Forty-five years. That's a long time. This guy must have all the wisdom. He probably knows everything there is to know about marriage and relationships...*

To be sure, he probably does know a lot. But be careful. This guy might not be the relationship expert you think he is.

Longevity in a relationship or a marriage does not automatically make someone an expert. Because when men like this speak, what kind of stuff do they inevitably say?

- "There were some challenging seasons."
- "There were a lot of dark times."
- "We still struggle over things, even today."

Whenever I heard this, I always wondered if I was the only one in the room who wanted to interrupt and ask for a clarification. Just how long was that "challenging season"? Eight years? Eight years of unhappiness and problems and emotional conflict?

And then what? Was it solved? Probably not. He and his wife likely got tired of arguing about it, so the problem was swept under the rug, replaced by a simmering resentment always on low boil in the background.

The point of a relationship isn't to grind out the decades amidst fighting, arguments, drama, turmoil, and pain. The point is for two people to be happier and more fulfilled than if the relationship didn't exist. But since people are constantly developing and changing, it's natural to eventually grow apart—even if they're married and have kids together.

Therapy can be a big help here. Bringing in a licensed counselor to act as an objective third party can help dig to the root of many issues—even ones that don't have anything to do with religion or your deconversion.

However, if a couple is no longer getting from the relationship what they once did and it's come to the point of causing a lot of pain, it's time to consider ending it—again, *yes*, even if they're married and have kids together.

Sometimes the greatest mark of a successful relationship between two mature and fully realized adults is knowing when it's time to end it. We'll address that now.

Divorce

Divorce sucks because, depending on your situation, you could lose a chunk of money, investments, even your house, all because you no longer believe in an ancient Abrahamic religion. You don't deserve that kind of penalty for finally seeing through the religious smoke, but unfortunately it's the reality of our modern era.

There is no shame in divorce. The Church teaches you to believe that divorce is a tragic, world-ending, soul-crushing Armageddon that could have been avoided had the couple been more focused on God.

That is completely wrong. This teaching has kept so many people in toxic relationships and marriages that should never have lasted as long as they did.

A healthy divorce happens when two grown, mature people have developed and changed and no longer feel they are best served by proceeding forward together.

Perhaps they are realizing for the first time that they never should have gotten married in the first place.

If this happens to you, then you need to handle the legal aspects of your divorce as quickly as possible. Spend some time learning the details of divorce in your state or country and interview some divorce attorneys. Once that's done, the material laid out in previous sections of this book become doubly important for landing back on your feet again.

If you find yourself newly single, circle back to the top of this section and read it again. Although it's written toward younger guys, it now applies to you—especially the points about building yourself up to the man you were always supposed to be.

Conclusion

Men are obsessed with women. That might seem basic, but it's true. The natural desire that a man has to have sex with women is one of the most powerful forces on earth. Men spend a huge amount of time thinking about how they can meet, hook up, and have relationships with the women they find attractive.

But however powerful the impulse, this should not be your priority.

If you've read and are starting to address the issues raised in the previous sections in this book, imagine what your life could look like:

- You are making decent money from numerous diversified income sources that you own and control.

- You are strong, fast, and athletic.
- You are skilled in one or more interesting hobbies.
- You have a rewarding relationship with your family.
- You have a strong social network of men who build you up and help you improve.

If all of those things are true, you won't have to try very hard to get a woman to like you.

Invest in yourself *first*. Accomplish everything you want in life *first*. Become the ideal version of yourself *first*. Women and relationships will follow.

Chapter 11
YOUR SPIRITUALITY

> *"The greater our knowledge increases the more our ignorance unfolds."* — John F. Kennedy

When I moved overseas to work and live, one of my main goals was meeting and getting to know people with different belief systems than mine. Since I was moving to the Middle East, I assumed I'd be meeting a lot of Muslims, and I did. I also met a lot of atheists, and a lot of Christians. Christianity, particularly Catholicism, was surprisingly well-represented.

But there was one lady who stood out from all the rest. Her name was Jane. She was a colleague and we worked closely together for a long time. As I got to know her, she started telling me more and more about her spirituality and what she believed. And she wasn't shy about it.

She believed in "the Universe," the "Law of Attraction," past lives, reincarnation, and even more concepts that were totally new to me at the time. She told me she saw spirits and that she had family members who were clairvoyants (people who claim to interact with the spiritual world through extrasensory perception).

She explained to me how she had done past life regression therapy to learn about the people her soul used to inhabit—a man in ancient Greece and a tribal Arab girl. She believed that the soul continues on after we die and that we'll eventually inhabit new bodies—even ones from past history since, to her, time was not linear.

She told me of a man she consulted with regularly who would use astrology and the location of the planets to make broad predictions and warnings about her immediate future. She had just picked up horseback riding, and when this man configured her star chart, he told her that she should avoid horses for the time being, supposedly without any foreknowledge of her new hobby. Jane promptly quit her equestrian class.

She wrote affirmations about the positive future of our workplace and hid them around the department. I once watched her use a pendulum to try to predict who would be chosen as our next supervisor.

I surprised myself in all these interactions with her. I thought I would put up a wall, stop listening, or call her crazy. But I never thought she was crazy. Instead, I was fascinated. Even though her beliefs didn't really resonate with me, I could still understand her point of view and how she came to the conclusion that this was the way the world and the universe worked.

What the Church Teaches You About Spirituality

The Church positions itself as the absolute authority over your spiritual life. It hands you all the answers. If there are no clear answers, then the solution is to simply "have faith." You are also commanded to believe a series of far-fetched claims, such that Jesus was born of a virgin and that he rose from the dead three days after he was crucified. Entertaining any spiritual beliefs outside the standard doctrine—such as the things Jane believed—is sinful and wrong, even if they're harmless.

Perhaps the most egregious issue with the church's control over your spirituality is that it suppresses your childlike sense of wonder by handing down answers, as unsatisfying as they are, to all of life's great mysteries. When you look up at the night sky and see the constellations and galaxies? God made that. When you wonder about the human experience and how we're all after the same things despite our cultural differences? God made us. Or how everything is interconnected via physics, chemistry, math, music, and art, and the things we've learned about our world and universe and all the coming discoveries in the future—God gets all the credit.

Cold, Hard Science

"Occam's razor" is a well-known principle among both atheists and agnostics who get into debates with Christians, even though William of Ockham believed in God.[1] It can be paraphrased as follows: "the simplest solution is most likely the correct one." Atheists love Occam's razor because it's an easy way to take down the supernatural claims of the Bible, which believers have no way of proving.

Usually when a man deconverts, his next philosophical step is to believe in nothing but cold, hard science. If science can't prove it, it's not to be taken seriously. When we've been traumatized by our religion, it's only natural to flee to a completely antithetical school of thought for cover and protection. I fully understand why someone like this would take shelter under the umbrella of cold, hard science, maybe for the rest of their lives.

But before we head into the final chapters of this book and the beginning of your new life as a deconverted man, humor me for a few moments longer.

Wonder and Curiosity

One of the best books I've ever read is a biography of Leonardo da Vinci by Walter Isaacson. Isaacson approached the Renaissance Era polymath as he was—a lowborn, everyday guy, and yet in modern times, we've built Da Vinci up to be some sort of superhuman genius. I thought the same until I read Isaacson's book.

Da Vinci was just as prone to distraction and failure as any of us. Many of his paintings are unfinished simply because he lost interest. His notebooks show his attempts to learn Latin, but he never made any meaningful progress and spoke only Italian throughout his life. His documented experiments in the realms of anatomy, mathematics, and machinery showed that he was thinking correctly but incorrect in his execution or missing key details. Many of his potential discoveries and breakthroughs were actually achieved by others years later.

Isaacson painted the picture (pun intended) of a man who was not gifted, but *curious*. He asked questions, sought answers through experimentation, and wrote down what he'd learned. By doing this, he was able to make connections that his contemporaries weren't making between seemingly unrelated things. Artists back then didn't study cadavers, for example, which gave Leonardo's paintings a much more truthful representation of people and animals than his rival, Michelangelo.[2]

Da Vinci's life was a revelation to me, and I implore you not to disregard your curiosity. Open your mind, wonder about everything, ask questions and experiment. Our world and our universe are big and complex. How boring it would be to never wonder about them.

Fundamentalists are among the least curious people there are since they already have all the answers. They know where the earth and the universe came from. They know where people came from. They know the meaning of life. And they know what happens after we die.

All of this is taught to young children in Sunday school; some will never question any of it for the rest of their lives.

But here's the kicker: If we criticize Christians, we should also take a hard look at ourselves as well. Atheists who only believe in cold, hard science can sometimes fall into beliefs and practices that are as dogmatic and absolute as those of the fundamentalists they attack.

Listen to people whose beliefs would be considered absurd by the scientific community. That person likely didn't pull his opinions out of thin air—he probably came to them through some kind of experience. Just because it hasn't been validated by science (yet) doesn't mean it has no value. Be open to what you might learn from them. What have you got to lose?

As a former fundamentalist, you likely spent all your time living with a closed, made-up mind with answers that were never questioned. Now is your chance to strike out on your own and seek the truths that resonate the most *for you*.

Switching Organized Religions

This is rare, but it does happen. I have a very good friend who converted to Islam later in her life. And I stand by what I said about keeping an open mind and seeking your truth. But switching from one organized religion to another seems like a lateral pass in football. It does not advance your position.

Your number one focus of deconversion should be *progressive change* in all things—your lifestyle, your thoughts, and your actions. Do what you feel you must to move forward in your life, but keep in mind that when it comes to the organized religions of the world, the grass is not always greener on the other side—it is simply different, but no less dogmatic.

Meditation and Mindfulness

You hear it all the time these days: You need to be meditating. Meditation has broken into the mainstream in a big way. I might even call it a fad.

Apps like Headspace or Sam Harris's "Waking Up" have endeavored to bring meditation and mindfulness to the masses and, for the most part, the masses have eaten it up. Sometimes, though, the reason given to practice meditation and mindfulness is incomplete—its biggest draw seems to be a promise to reduce stress. And that's appealing. If you're stressed, this seems like a simple enough solution to combat it. If it doesn't work, you haven't wasted much time.

To me, though, meditation and mindfulness are about so much more than "reducing stress." Rather, they are about reclaiming control of your own brain. What, you may be wondering, does it mean to lose control of my own brain? Chances are you have and not yet realized it.

- When your phone dings with a text message you weren't expecting, are you able to just leave it in your pocket or on the table or do you immediately pick it up and see who it's from?
- When CNN blares "Breaking news!" and starts talking about the latest thing the president has tweeted, do you stay glued to the tube or are you able to walk away?
- When you finish a YouTube video or Netflix episode and the countdown to the next episode begins, are you able to turn it off and do something else or do you let the content keep rolling?

We've all been victims of the above or similar distractions at some point in our lives. But if you find that it's a habitual pattern, you may not have as firm a control on your mind as you think you do.

It's not completely your fault. News sites, social media, and online shopping websites have all been designed with human psychology in mind. They know how to addict you, to keep you scrolling. They know when and how to feed you hits of dopamine that keep you coming back for more.

Your mind and your focus can be trained just like any other muscle in the body. Only after you begin such training do you realize how valuable they are and start to understand just how much of your attention you give away to mindless media content and internet surfing. Additionally, when you reclaim your mind and your focus, you are better able to commit more time to investing in yourself.

Here is how to meditate:

- Find a quiet place free from major distractions. Minor sounds are okay, and can even help you practice. You don't need to worry about a ticking clock, a running refrigerator, or traffic noises outdoors.
- Set a timer if you want. If you use your phone, make sure to silence it. At first, set the timer for five minutes. As you practice, keep increasing the time. Thirty minutes is a good goal, although some people can sit for far longer.
- Sit on the floor lotus style or on a comfortable chair. Keep your back straight. Rest your palms on your thighs. You can either close your eyes or keep them open.
- Take a deep breath in through your nose and let it out through either your nose or mouth. Breathe deep enough so that it fills and expands your abdomen.

- As best as you can, keep your mind focused on your breath. To aid this, you can count them, one through ten, and then start over again. Alternatively, you can think the words "in" during the inhale and "out" during the exhale. This is my preference since I often lose count and that causes a distraction.
- If you catch your mind wandering or you start thinking about something else besides following your breath, gently let the thought go and return your focus to the breath.

The first time you do this will reveal a lot about the state of your mind. I had a really hard time focusing on my breath during those five minutes. My monkey mind was crazy with thoughts—things that were stressing me, things I had to do that day, little reminders of this and that such as remembering to do the dishes.

It was clear I had a lot of work to do on my mind. My desire was to be still and focus on one thing (my breath) and yet dozens of other things intruded against my will. No wonder I was mentally exhausted and emotionally drained at the end of each day. I realized that I didn't have control over my own brain and knew I had to change.

I committed to doing the above meditation exercise every day. I also increased the length of time as I improved. As a result, I became a lot more aware of my thoughts and emotions—especially the ones that crept into my head uninvited.

If someone did something unintentionally that pissed me off, I was able to recognize that thought before I emotionally reacted to it. I had also developed the skill to let it go. If I wanted to dedicate my focus to something mentally taxing (such as writing this book), I was better able to ignore my phone and other notification dings on my computer.

My focus and my attention were mine again.

I am no meditation expert, and if you've had a meditation practice for a while, you are much more advanced than I am. Great! Keep it up!

I do believe this practice has earned its place in the lifestyle and routine of any deconverted man as a way of seizing back control of his mind. Deconverting can be an emotional and angry time, and as I said earlier, it's in your best interest to get through this phase as quickly as possible. Meditation and being mindful of your thoughts and emotions from moment to moment is a valuable tool to help you do this.

Affirmations

An affirmation is a statement that reflects a goal you have for improving your life and future. During meditation is an excellent time to repeat them to yourself like a mantra or listen to a recording of them. Here are some examples of affirmations:

- *I am financially secure and can afford anything I want.*
- *I am an adventurous traveler who has many rich experiences in exciting locations around the world.*
- *I am muscular and athletic and eat only healthy food.*

Notice the wording: "I am," not "I want" or "I want to be." It's important to design your mantras to state your desired truth in the present tense. Why? Your subconscious mind, unlike your conscious mind, is highly malleable and suggestible. When you repeat these mantras over and over in a meditative state as if they are already happening, they sink deeply into your subconscious mind, activating forces that will help make them a reality.

Simply repeating the words won't bring about the necessary change. You will eventually need to take action, and under these conditions you will because your subconscious mind now considers the content of your mantra as part of your identity. You will begin to act in accordance to the identity that you are claiming.

This practice is valuable for a deconverted man because this same technique was used against you in the Church for the opposite effect. Do these "reverse affirmations" sound familiar?

- Your good deeds are filthy rags.
- You are nothing without Jesus.
- You were born a sinner, and the only thing you can do is rely on God's grace.

A lot of negativity is used by the Church to keep you obedient and dependent on God. Even after deconverting, many of these damaging messages may still be operating inside your subconscious and affecting the way you view yourself and the world around you. So it's time to write down some new mantras! Keep them in the present tense. Keep them positive. Align them with your goals and with your vision of who you want to be. Record them and listen to them while you meditate or as you are falling asleep at night. That way, they have the best chance of drifting into your subconscious mind.

Visualizations

Visualizations work in a similar way but instead of using words they are mental projections of the person you want to become. Follow the steps outlined in the section on meditation, but instead of keeping your mind focused on your breath, imagine yourself as who you want to be or *doing* what you want to achieve.

It helps to visualize yourself accomplishing a specific goal you've set for yourself. Make it vivid, even a little bit outlandish. *Feel* the emotions you expect to have while experiencing this future state. Here are some examples:

- Imagine yourself achieving your bench press goal. Feel yourself pushing out that final rep, chest muscles burning. Your spotter isn't touching the bar and is cheering you on. When you lock out your elbows and rack the bar, you stand up victorious.
- Imagine yourself on stage performing the songs you've written. See the crowds and hear them singing along. Feel the satisfaction of knowing your music has reached and impacted the masses.
- Imagine yourself working the job or owning the business that provides you with the money you need to live your dream life. Feel the comfort and security of having enough money where

you don't need to worry. Experience the confidence that comes with having a firm handle on your financial life.

As with affirmations, your church probably used the same visualization techniques I've described to influence your thoughts and behavior, especially if you had a pastor who was a gifted speaker. Just off the top of my head, here are some visualizations I've endured:

- A pastor asking us to close our eyes and visualize God on this throne, looking down at us on earth, urging us to run into his open arms for salvation.
- Graphic descriptions of Jesus's crucifixion and death to inspire guilt when we sin against him.
- Vivid imagery of hell to scare people (usually children) into accepting Jesus.
- Exploitative testimonies from visiting missionaries about squalid conditions in overseas countries to solicit donations to their organization.

If you can relate to these, then you remember how powerful it was. Utilize this same technique for your own benefit on your own terms.

The Law of Attraction

Affirmations and visualizations work because of the Law of Attraction. This "law" has been written about, with varying terminology, for centuries and with different levels of "spiritualization" attached. It has also been much maligned, and often fairly in my opinion. When some spiritual guru claims you can just sit around and daydream about the kind of future you want and it'll appear one day, they are misleading you.

Your affirmations and visualizations manifest themselves when combined with pertinent action. They instill a goal inside your mind that then spurs you into action toward accomplishing it.

Thinking about bench-pressing 300 pounds doesn't make you suddenly able to do it. It does, however, encourage you to go to the gym and add weight to the bar incrementally until you eventually work up to your goal. And holding that image in your mind does seem to accelerate your progress.

Who you are is defined by what you do, and what you do is influenced by what you think about. You rarely take meaningful actions without first thinking about them.

- Evangelical Christians spend a lot of time thinking about Jesus and visualizing themselves going into the world and converting people with the power of the gospel.
- Megachurch pastors spend a lot of time visualizing themselves preaching to tens of thousands of people every Sunday.
- Youth pastors spend a lot of time visualizing themselves relating to and connecting with their church's younger generation.

Likewise, if you literally never think about the gym, you are unlikely to ever go. That is why the Law of

Attraction works. Once you alter what you think about and visualize, you will naturally change what you do. What you do—your new actions—define the new person that you will become. Your thoughts guide you to take the required actions to bring about your desired outcome.

This concept has been explored in much more depth in the books *Maximum Achievement* by Brian Tracy and the classic *Think and Grow Rich* by Napoleon Hill. I strongly recommend both.

Spiritual Transition

So far this book has been down to earth, rational, and practical. In my day-to-day life, I tend to be quite cerebral and pragmatic. But I also have an open mind and a curious nature. So allow me a moment to get a little "woo-woo" on you.

What I'm about to describe was very personal experience. When I went through it, I did not know what was happening to me and I wondered if I was normal. I took to the internet and discovered multiple sources confirming all of my symptoms as if they were reading my mind.

Wanting to further confirm, I even spoke to my friend Jane—the same one I mentioned at the beginning of this chapter—about what I was experiencing. She didn't blink an eye. She told me I was going through a spiritual transition.

A what?

Basically, a spiritual transition is when everything about you is changing all at once: Your mind, your thoughts, what you enjoy, who you enjoy being around, what you want to do, and most importantly, who you want to be. As a result, everything just seems off. Sometimes way off. You feel *disconnected*. Here are a few specifics:

Things that I used to love doing no longer interested me.

I found them boring or unfulfilling. I only wanted to engage in activities that were more of an investment in my future. Hanging out with friends and watching UFC (Ultimate Fighting Championship) hardly counted as that. I now preferred to read an educational nonfiction book.

The people I knew, even longtime friends, began to feel like they no longer belonged in my life.

I couldn't put a finger on why. They hadn't made me mad. They weren't annoying. They weren't insulting me or discouraging me or being rude. I just spontaneously began to feel like I wanted to be around different types of people.

I felt a strong desire to be alone.

Riding off the previous point, I began to isolate myself. At first, I didn't even know I was doing it. For some reason, I developed a strong desire to be alone in my quiet apartment, either reading or listening to podcasts. I would even silence my cell phone and leave it in the other room.

My job started to bother me when it never had before.

Not just my job, but my entire career. I started to wonder if I was really doing what I truly wanted to be doing. That's a bit scarier than just getting annoyed at my job because I can always find another one. Questioning my entire career choice was intense.

I could no longer watch violence in movies or TV shows.

I'd never been squeamish about this before but again, for unknown reasons, I could no longer tolerate it. I had to look away. Sometimes I even turned off the show and never finished it.

I wanted a hard reset.

I had a strong desire to uproot every aspect of my life and start anew. I wasn't even sure what I would do instead, but that was part of the draw.

I questioned everything.

Not just religious dogma but *everything*. Was there another job or career I would be better at than what I was doing? Why did I choose that career in the first place? How much of my life did I actually choose or was most of it chosen for me by well-meaning parents and teachers?

And there was more.

- A well-intentioned friend would tell me I should do something. Why?
- My boss would tell me there was a new

protocol in place for me to follow. Why?
- The U.S. president would declare a nation or world leader a threat. Why?

I pretty much demanded an explanation for everything.

I saw repeating number patterns everywhere.

This was the final straw. That's when I knew I had to speak to my friend Jane.

While all the above began happening, I found that at least once a day, such as when I checked the time on my phone, it would be 11:11 or 1:11 or 4:44. By far, the most common was 11:11. This wasn't confined only to random time checks, though.

- I met someone whose birthday was November 11 (11/11).
- I was in an office building and asked for directions, only to be sent to room 1111.
- The number 1111 appeared on new advertising signs on routes I drove often.
- I received a text from a friend at precisely 11:11 at night, asking to call them because it was important. It turned out to be *very* important.

Googling this phenomenon was what led me to discover that all the other symptoms went hand in hand with repeating number patterns. I was exposed to the idea of a spiritual transition for the first time.

I well understand that cognitive bias can be used to

explain this. However, I had read nothing about numerology prior to this and didn't know the number eleven had any kind of significance to spiritual practitioners. It was something I happened to notice on my own, and when it finally occurred to me to Google it, I found out I was far from the only person having these experiences. When I spoke to Jane about it, she shared with me all the significant times in her life when the number 11 had appeared to her in unusual ways.

I'm not talking about a bad day or even a bad week—this gradual change took place over the course of about three or four months. I also discovered that this is something that eventually happens to most people whether they realize what is happening or not. All at once, and in every part of their lives, they feel like they are in the wrong place or inhabiting the wrong body or living the wrong kind of life.

The feeling can be described as a general restlessness that beckons you to just *get out* of your current situation or circumstances.

I'm discussing it here because there is a high chance that you will go through the same thing as part of your deconversion. When people deconvert, it often results in a change of everything, not just your religious beliefs. If you haven't experienced this yet—or never do—that's fine. But remember this section if you start to go through something similar in the future.

If you aren't buying what I'm selling in this section, no worries. If you think I'm being too "woo-woo" and prefer to call such trying times by more palatable names (i.e., a mid-life crisis), I'm cool with that. The important thing is not what you call it but how you handle it.

What do you do during this time? Don't panic; just listen. Sometimes you have to step back and pay attention to what your heart and your gut are telling you.

I believe there is a guiding force inside all of us that we struggle to explain. Until now, we called it God. Whatever you call it now—your heart, gut, soul, intuition, the Universe—it is urging you toward your greater good. Don't fight it. Be patient with yourself.

Cheesy, I know, but sometimes the cheesy stuff is the answer. It pains me to admit that not every problem can be bashed through with only intellectual, rational force. And deconversion *can* be very distressing; you can experience a lot of loss and confusion as you shed your old skin. But the new you will be closer to the person you were always meant to become.

Your Spiritual Journey

In his book *The Hero with a Thousand Faces*, mythologist-author Joseph Campbell describes "the hero's journey" (also called the monomyth) that underlies most great stories and legends throughout human history. It includes elements that are common to most timeless tales—elements that humans have identified with for generations.

The hero's journey was traditionally about a man who starts off comfortably living in the "Normal World" where everything is as he is accustomed to. Then an "Inciting Incident" forces him from his status quo and onto a journey. At first, the Hero refuses the "Call to Adventure." He is afraid or feels unprepared or unworthy. He doesn't want to give up the comfort of the Normal World. Eventually, the Hero decides to leave the Normal World and cross into the New World, which is very different from the world he is used to.

As the Hero ventures forth, he encounters trials and obstacles. Some of them are external, such as enemies who seek to defeat him. Some are internal, such the Hero's feelings of inadequacy which are also capable of defeating him. Along the way, the Hero is aided by allies and guided by a mentor who has already been through what the Hero is starting.

Before the Hero can complete his journey, he must undergo a crushing defeat or major setback that threatens to destroy him. The Hero must then use all he's learned from his journey to overcome this setback and ultimately defeat his enemies, the most important of which are usually the ones inside him. The Hero then returns to his Normal World but is forever changed by what he went through. He will never be the same again.

If this structure sounds familiar, it's because many classic stories such as *Star Wars*, *Harry Potter*, and *Lord of the Rings* are based on the hero's journey.

It can be helpful to visualize your deconversion as your own hero's journey. Perhaps your deconversion was the Inciting Incident that drove you from your Normal World. I imagine you refused the Call to Adventure for a time by trying to force yourself to remain a believer. Ultimately, however, there was no turning back as you entered your New World. And yes, there will be trials, obstacles, and roadblocks. There will be enemies, both external and internal. You will also meet allies and mentors.

This image and affirmation will come in especially

handy when, toward the end of your journey, you encounter a major setback—that moment when you feel like defeat is imminent and all is lost. You now know that this moment is not where the hero's journey—*your* story—ends. According to the monomyth, this moment is the final test. You will break through to the other side victorious, stronger, wiser, changed, and prepared to mentor the next wave of heroes who will follow in your steps.

Conclusion

After losing his religion, every deconverted man will land somewhere on the broad spectrum of spirituality. Some will sit staunchly in the camp of cold, hard science while others will embrace the esoteric side of humanity's unanswered questions. Both are fine, and so is everything in between.

The key is to keep revisiting the state of your spiritual beliefs. Reevaluate. Ask different questions. Talk to new people and see what they think. If you feel that nothing changes, then no problem. But one day you may surprise yourself.

Think back to when you were "saved." You confessed that Jesus Christ was your Lord and Savior, the Son of God, who had died for your sins and been resurrected on the third day. Remember how deeply you believed it, and for how long, and how you were convinced that you were right and would never change your mind.

Look at you now. Your spiritual life has changed immensely. There is no reason to believe that it can't change again.

PART III

Chapter 12

YOUR LIFE

"Change is the end result of all true learning." — Leo Buscaglia

You've come this far and you're probably thinking one thing: "This is a ton of stuff! How am I supposed to get all this done?"
You get it done by flipping switches.

Flipping Switches

Imagine each one of the seven life areas we've discussed as a switch similar to a light switch. At the start of your deconversion journey, they are all turned off. Now pick only two. Maybe even one, but no more than two. Two is the maximum you should work on at one time. This will keep you from getting overwhelmed. You'll make faster and more meaningful progress.

You are now committed to rebuilding those particular

areas of your post-deconversion life. You have also committed to temporarily ignoring the other life areas.

Let's say you've switched on Health and Relationships with Women. Here's how your life will look:

You start by rereading those corresponding sections and making a plan which consists of goals. These goals are chosen by you and no one else. It's about what you want.

Let's say you want a more muscular, masculine body. Great. You research a muscle-building training program that will have you in the gym three times a week. Then you go out and join a gym. You throw away all your potato chips and energy drinks and replace them with quality protein, vegetables, and water. You then implement your plan. You go to the gym, you eat your healthy food, and you watch your body change.

With the other switch, you break up with your girlfriend who keeps nagging and guilting you about coming back to church. Then you stay single for a few months while you're on your training program. Once those muscles start to show, your confidence increases, so you go back out into the world to meet new women (or get on dating sites or apps). For the next few weeks or so, you date many different women. Eventually, you will find a girl you like and she becomes your new girlfriend. You can now flip the Relationships with Women switch off.

Your Health switch is still on, though, and will remain so as you actively build your ideal body. But you now have room for one more life area. You decide to flip on the Money switch.

Now you can re-purpose the time you spent looking for a new girlfriend on making more money. The nights of the week that were once dedicated to dating are now dedicated to building an income source that serves a targeted market that you are able to bring value to.

As you're ramping up your income source, you finally hit your strength goals, so you decide to flip off the Health switch. That doesn't mean you stop going to the gym. It means you stop focusing on *new* strength goals and instead go to the gym simply to maintain the body you've already built.

With this new space available, you flip on the Social Life switch and dedicate the time left from your Health pursuits to seeking new male friendships that will inspire you and build you up. Once you've found those friends, you can flip that switch off and simply maintain those friendships while you actively improve something else.

And so on.

Goals

After you flip a switch, how do you decide when to turn it off? When you reach the goal you set for yourself.

Goals are interesting. If you've never been a goal setter, it may take some time to learn this skill—yes, it's a skill. If you regularly set goals for yourself, then you know how much of a positive impact they can have on your daily life.

Everyone in the Church generally has the same goals, which are influenced by the pastor and other members of the congregation. Below is a common list of goals I was instructed to have while in the Church, almost all of which I failed:

- Read my Bible more.
- Have a quiet time every morning.
- Pray more.
- Spend more time preparing for Bible study.

In most instances, these goals were converted into vague prayer requests, and you know how I feel about that. Basically, I turned the goals over to God and expected him to magically make them happen.

The only real goal that I kept during my time in the Church was to finally read the entire Bible by the end of the year, which I mentioned in Chapter 1. I didn't know it at the time, but the reason I accomplished this goal was because it was a SMART goal.

I didn't invent the idea of SMART. If you've worked for an employer for a reasonable length of time, it's likely that, at some point, they've brought in a productivity consultant, rounded up you and your colleagues, and taught you all how to make SMART goals. This happened to me but I spaced out because I understood that the goals these people wanted me to create were meant to benefit the company, not my own life.

However, that doesn't mean SMART goals don't work. They do. That's why entire consulting firms have been built around it.

SMART stands for Specific, Measurable, Attainable, Relevant, Time-based. Using my example of reading the entire Bible in a year, we can break down that goal using this standard:

- Specific: Read all 66 books of the Bible.

- Measurable: Of the 66 books of the Bible, there are 1,189 chapters. There are 365 days in the year. That means I need to read 3 or 4 chapters per day to complete the goal.
- Attainable: There are 783,137 words in the Bible. I've read entire fiction book series in less than a year that contain far more words than that. I can definitely pull this off.
- Relevant: I don't want to be a Christian who hasn't read the book that's the basis of my entire religion. That weakens my testimony.
- Time-based: This will be done before the end of the year.

Compare all that to the way most people in the Church word their goals. It's no wonder no one sticks with anything when all they say is, "Read the Bible more often."

When you define your goals and methods using the SMART framework, it makes them very clear and very real. It also gives you a definite end point, a finish line to strive for. When goals like this are firmly inserted into your subconscious mind, you are far more likely to achieve them.

So when you decide to flip the switch of one of your life areas, you will need one or two clearly defined goals. Once you hit them, you can consider flipping the switch off. In the case of your health, here's an example of a good goal:

"I squat twice my bodyweight. I will accomplish this in one year. I weigh 150 pounds, so my goal is to be able to squat 300 pounds for at least one repetition. I can currently squat 200 pounds. If I add two pounds a week for a year, I will hit my goal. I need to increase my squat because, beginning next year, I will compete in powerlifting competitions."

- Specific: I squat twice my bodyweight.
- Measurable: I weigh 150 pounds, so my goal is to lift 300 pounds.
- Attainable: If I add two pounds a week for a year, I will hit my goal.
- Relevant: I need to be stronger because I will compete in powerlifting competitions.
- Time-based: I will accomplish this in one year.

Write Down Your Goals

Have you ever made New Year's resolutions and forgotten about them by February? Of course you have. We've all done that.

When goals remain in your head only, they are nothing more than thoughts, easily lost in the thousands of other thoughts you have in a day. You need to pay the heating bill. You need to pick up milk from the grocery store on the way home. You need to reply to a client email.

On top of all those thoughts come the events that take up even more space in your mental inventory. You catch the flu. The company you work for announces that it's downsizing. Your girlfriend breaks up with you.

As life progresses, your days become all about extinguishing the small fires that spring up. Your goals, the things you actually *want* to do, get relegated to "someday." That's when all this crap quiets down. When life gets calmer. When the economy gets more stable. When the kids move out.

Good luck with that. It's not how life works. There is always something that demands your immediate attention. It is therefore your job to keep your goals a priority and in the front of your mind. The best way to do this is to write them down, ideally in a personal journal. You can also write them on index cards you put by your computer at work or on sticky notes you attach to your bathroom mirror.

Better yet, rewrite them in the morning after you wake up and at night before you go to bed. Recall what we discussed earlier about getting things into your subconscious. This writing and rewriting of your goals keeps them in your thoughts, and your thoughts guide your actions.

Your New Life

Your ultimate objective is building your seven life areas to a point where they are optimized to your satisfaction and serve you in terms of your happiness and freedom. You need to get those areas to a place where "flipping the switch" is no longer necessary, where you can simply enjoy them and the fruits of the labor they produce for you.

Ideally, to keep them fresh, you find a way to keep them active every week for the rest of your life. Here's an example:

Every day: meditate; work; spend time with (or call) your family.

Every three days: exercise; go on a date with your girlfriend or spouse.

Once a week: grab dinner and drinks with your buddies; participate in or practice your hobby.

Once you become a happy, free, and well-balanced man, you will find very little reason to look back on your days in fundamentalist religion and how it hurt you. Even more exciting, you are now a man of means, support, clarity, health, and discipline. You've shaped yourself into the man you were always meant to be. The next step is to go out and leave your impact on the world, shaping your local or global community in ways you know you can help. More about that in the next chapter.

This is literally the opposite of how fundamentalists go about their lives. They prioritize the world before building themselves, which severely limits the amount of impact they can hope to have. Fortunately, this no longer describes you. You're different now. You're better.

Tying it All Together

We've come a long way but a key piece of this puzzle is still missing.

You've accumulated a lot of information about what you need to do.

You hopefully have a clear understanding of why you need to do these things.

But there is another level that answers the question of "Why" more deeply and clearly. *Why* build yourself into a better man? *Why* prioritize healing from the damage caused by religion? If we only become dust when we die, what's the point of doing anything at all?

The next chapter will answer these questions and tie together everything you've learned. It's possibly the most important chapter in this book.

Chapter 13

YOUR MISSION

> *"Here is the test to find whether your mission on Earth is finished: if you're alive, it isn't."* — Richard Bach

Let me introduce you to Alex. Actually, I don't need to introduce you because you already know him. There's an "Alex" in every church in the world. Maybe it was you.

Alex is an early-twenties guy who's *on fire* for the Lord. Alex goes to Uganda one summer on a mission trip. He's there for *six whole weeks*! During that time, his Facebook and Instagram accounts are flooded with photos of him and African village children. You don't know what exactly he's doing over there (except taking pictures with a bunch of Ugandan kids) but it sure looks like the Lord's work.

At the end of those six weeks, Alex returns home. He is pulled up on stage before the sermon on Sunday and speaks for the entire Uganda team. He shares about all the powerful ways God is moving in Uganda, blessing the people there, and how God is changing lives throughout Africa.

Proudly and boldly, in front of everyone, Alex declares that God has laid Uganda on his heart. He has fallen in love with the country, its people, and their culture, and he has a desire to lead them to the Lord. He asserts that he *will* go back, this time as a team leader, and invites everyone to pray with him (and donate money toward the next trip).

One small problem. Because the church has other regularly scheduled mission trips to Mexico (to build houses), to Europe (because despite the cathedrals on every street corner, the people still haven't heard about Jesus), and to China (where all missionaries have "tricked" the Chinese government about why they are there), there won't be another trip to Uganda until next summer.

That's fine, Alex thinks. He can wait. Until then, he'll support the local Ugandan churches through prayer and giving.

But time goes on. Alex gets busy with work. He has bills like everyone else, so his donations to Uganda get "postponed." He loses touch with the partner church because other American churches have swept in to get their pictures with the children.

Next summer rolls around. It's time to sign up for the annual Uganda mission trip. Alex is asked by his pastor if he's going. He says yes at first but quickly realizes his summer is quite busy. He's joined an Ultimate Frisbee league and they have games every weekend.

Also, six weeks is a long time to take off from his job. He's already spent most of his vacation time on a trip to Cancun with the guys in his Bible study.

Alex decides he'll go next summer.

But that fall, Alex meets a girl and marries her early the next year. Now he's focused on his new married life. The Uganda trip passes again.

He promises to himself that he'll go back to Uganda *next* summer. He'll even bring his new wife. But then Alex and his wife have a baby. He definitely can't head to Uganda and leave his wife with a newborn for six whole weeks. After that year, it doesn't even occur to Alex to sign up for the Uganda trip.

He never goes again.

Does that story sound familiar? Every church across the world has members who once thought they "had a heart" for some mission-trip destination only for that passion to burn out faster than it started. Maybe you are guilty of that yourself.

The story ended that way because Alex didn't have a true mission. Real missions cannot be derailed by life circumstances, even big ones such as getting married or having a kid. Missions are as much a part of you as your own body and soul.

What is a true mission and how does it differ from the church's idea of a mission? This chapter—the most important one in this book—will examine that.

A Man on a Mission

If you've ever met a "man on a mission," you knew it. You knew it even if you didn't know what his specific Mission was.

Men with Missions give off a certain aura. It's a sense of assuredness that other men don't have, an energy that surrounds them and that others pick up on. This energy seems to say, "I'm building something. I'm on my way."

These men are usually normal guys with families, jobs, and homes, but there is *something else* that drives them to a point beyond what most men in the modern area achieve. This something else is ever present in their lives, driving their every action, every plan, and every goal. It's almost always bigger than them. To outside observers, it may even seem impossible. Not to these guys. They are powered by a determination that others envy, and by the time they're on their death beds, they will have made a dent in the world.

That *something else* is your Mission. It is the purpose of your life. It is the reason you live. It is the *why* to your *what*.

It is vital that all men have a Mission. As men, we are natural doers, creators, movers, and shakers. We are driven to accomplish, conquer, claim, and establish. These traits are born from the testosterone that flows in our veins. Unfortunately, the modern era doesn't have much use for the natural tendencies of men. The world has been explored. There is no need for hunters and gatherers. No invading tribe is coming after our own.

That's okay. There is still plenty of work to be done to make the world a better place. *A lot* of work. There is still room for men who have Missions.

What the Church Teaches You About Missions

The term "mission," when used in regard to the Church, is synonymous with going overseas and evangelizing locals in foreign countries. But that's not the whole story.

Churches themselves even say there is a lot more to "mission work" than that.

In the context of churches, I put the word "mission" in quotes because the missions of the Church are not real missions.

Think back to all the conversations you had with other Christians. Most, if not all of them, went on and on about how Christianity, God, Jesus, and the Church gave them a sense of purpose. Maybe it also gave you a sense of purpose and now you're struggling after deconverting because you feel that your life no longer has meaning.

People who derive their sense of purpose from the Church often get to choose from only a preselected number of church-approved "missions"—as if being limited to shopping down only one aisle in the grocery store. Here are some examples:

- Be a head pastor.
- Be a youth pastor.
- Be a worship leader.
- Be a rousing Christian speaker.
- Be a missionary.

Maybe you identify with one or more of the items on that list. Perhaps you remember choosing one of those paths for your own life when you believed, and the loss of that life path has left you feeling empty.

I get it. I've been there. But it's important to understand that those pre-selected and pre-approved Church paths are not true missions. Here's why:

They are chosen for you by someone else.

Maybe it was your pastor, an overbearing parent, or a highly opinionated girlfriend. Chances are, you chose the path you did because you felt it was something you *should* do, not something you actually *wanted* to do.

This was then exacerbated by all the external praise you received, further helping convince you that you were doing what "God called you to do."

Many others, perhaps thousands of others, are already doing the same thing.

How many pastors are there? How many missionaries are in Asia? How many mediocre guitar players are trying to be in the next Hillsong?

A true Mission that impacts the world for the greater good is something only *you* can do. You bring a distinct voice and perspective to the world, even if you don't feel that's true. Your unique experiences add value where others cannot.

If God were real, he wouldn't need you to do this mission anyway.

If God is all-knowing and all-powerful, why does he need a bunch of flawed humans to bring about his kingdom? He could do it much more efficiently with a snap of his mighty fingers.

Working toward a church-based mission is literally a waste of time.

Finding Your Mission

We're used to seeing missions portrayed in movies and video games as epic conquests of villainous bad guys or rescuing damsels in distress. But those are only stories. We live and operate in the real world—which doesn't mean us regular guys can't also have a Mission.

In fact, not only *can* you have a Mission; you *should*.

Your Mission is what you are on this planet for. It's your purpose. It's what drives every action you take and every decision you make from the moment you get out of bed in the morning to when you go to sleep at night.

Your Mission isn't just *what* you do; it's *why* you do it and *who* you do it for. And yes, I am capitalizing the word "Mission" on purpose. It's that important.

The loss of a Mission is one of the biggest challenges deconverted men face. When they were members of the Church, their mission was clear: Reach people for God and bring about his kingdom. Now that it's gone, these men feel like they've lost all meaning and purpose in their lives.

In response, a lot of these guys go too far in the other direction. They start telling everyone they meet—usually online—that all life is meaningless. It's a nihilistic way to live and breeds a lot of unhappiness. I don't recommend it.

Instead, now that you are on the other side of religion, discover what your new Mission is. The best part is knowing that this new Mission is *your* Mission and yours alone. People in the Church are automatically assigned the mission of evangelizing whether they want to or not.

You didn't get to choose. Now you do. You get to live your true purpose.

Finding your life Mission may sound like serious business. It is. It's also something that will take some time. If you don't already have an idea of what your Mission is, don't expect it to come to you overnight. Some prep work is required, things like deep thought, prolonged contemplation, and possibly some epiphanies. This is your life Mission we're talking about. Whatever work is necessary will be worth the effort.

If it were easy, everyone would have their life Mission sorted out and no one would live aimlessly. Most people live without intention; they react to reality rather than purposely building their desired reality. Don't be one of those people. You'll be much happier in the long run.

I'll give you practical steps to guide you in rediscovering your Mission, but first you will need to make some preparations.

Wait for the Perfect Day

Do you like sunshine and blue skies? Wait for the weather to clear up. Do you find peace and tranquility in a rainstorm? Wait for the clouds to roll in. Does a light snowfall bring you peace? Wait for the flurries.

Get Your Mind and Mood Right

Even when your perfect day arrives, pause and take note of how you feel. Are you stressed about something? Has your boss said something that pissed you off? Do you feel generally down in the dumps? If so, wait. Don't go further until both your environment and your mind are right.

When we're dealing with something as serious as finding your Mission, you want all the factors to be optimized.

Leave the House

It's your perfect day and you're in a great mood. Excellent. Now, leave the house.

I'm sure your home brings you great comfort, but you need to leave. It has too many distractions. The reason you waited for your perfect day was to get out and enjoy it. Go somewhere that means a lot to you and preferably where you will be alone.

Bring a Pen and Paper

Do not use a computer or a tablet and definitely *don't use your phone*. Going analog improves your thinking and is more natural and human.[1] Although technology is convenient, there is a slight disconnect between man and machine.

Again, we want to optimize all variables when searching for your Mission. You can always transcribe what you write by hand into a word processor later.

Leave Your Phone in the Car

Don't bring your phone to your special place. That little box of distractions won't help you determine your Mission. If you must, tell your family or job that you'll be away from your phone for a few hours and that you will get back to them later in the day.

Imagine a Hard Reset of Your Life

This is an important step that will keep your search for a Mission *honest* and about *you* only.

Take some time to imagine a life where your family, friends, spouse, and kids don't exist. Gasp! How dare I suggest something so horrible? Just do it.

If any or all of these people are at the forefront of your mind when you're searching for your Mission, you risk formulating a Mission that is for them and not for you. There will be time to incorporate your loved ones later. For now, this is only *for you*.

Imagine You've Accomplished All Your Goals

Now imagine what your life would be like if you had accomplished all of your goals. Everything you've wanted to achieve, you've done. On top of that, you've mastered all the skills you've ever wanted to learn. You are effectively a "finished" man.

Imagine You Have 10 Million Dollars in the Bank

Cash. And this is what's left after you've already bought all the cars, boats, planes, and houses you've ever wanted.

Imagine that You Only Have Three Years Left to Live.

But anything you want to happen in those remaining years *will* come to fruition. You cannot fail.

Now that you've prepared yourself, you're ready to begin the work. Remember:

- You have no daily obligations that demand your immediate attention.
- All of your major life goals are accomplished.
- You've learned and mastered all the skills you'll ever need.
- You have all the money you'll ever need.
- You only have three years left to live.

What do you do now? It would be a shame for a superhuman to reach his peak and then spend the rest of his days playing video games. How do you give back? What do you give back? To whom do you give back? Or to borrow Church lingo—who or what do you have a heart for? What group, cause, or community do *you* care about that you feel a strong desire to change, affect, or influence?

Here are some practical steps to finding your life Mission:

Step 1: Determine Who

When choosing who you want to impact, it's best to focus on a broad community of people. Some good examples are:

1. Children
2. Special-needs adults

3. The elderly
4. Animals

Some bad examples are:

1. Your dad
2. Your spouse
3. Your sister

You may cringe when you read that, but it's true.

Remember, your Mission is something that guides your entire life and cannot be derailed. Basing your Mission on one specific person or a small group of people will leave it vulnerable, even if you love them very much. What if your spouse divorces you? What if your dad dies? Immediately, your Mission is rendered null and void and you're left once again without a guiding light in your life.

Defining your target in a broad sense will prevent this problem. Working with animals or "special needs" adults will never be finished or obsolete.

Step 2: Determine What

What will you do for this group of people you care about? You can't say, "I will solve all the problems for all elderly people." You need to be a bit more specific.

1. "I will build communities of play for children in foster care."
2. "I will help to expand the Special Olympics throughout the world."
3. "I will facilitate programs in retirement homes

across the country that keep elderly people active."
4. "I will work to decrease and prevent the poaching of endangered species."

These tasks may seem huge and unachievable. That's the point. Remember, in this brainstorming, you have no real limits to what you can achieve. And one the reasons they seem larger than life is because they are Missions you can never "finish."

Step 3: Determine How

Now that you know what you're going to do, you need to determine how you're going to do it. Remember, in this exercise, you have no limitations.

1. "I will use social media to reach out to foster parents around the country and plan events specifically for foster children."
2. "I will partner with relevant and influential organizations to bring special needs services to areas where they do not yet exist."
3. "I will connect personal trainers and physical therapists who have experience with elderly patients to develop programs for retirement communities."
4. "I will volunteer with and donate to local animal protection agencies around the world."

Step 4: Determine Why

This is the step that keeps you honest. Don't choose a group of people or something to do just because it seems noble. That's what people in the Church do because they feel guilty if they don't. You need a strong *why* behind the group *and* what you're planning to do for them. If you can't come up with a reason, then you're on the wrong path.

1. "I was a lonely foster child who struggled to make friends."
2. "My brother had special needs and he was happiest when he was competing with other people like him."
3. "My grandfather was an athlete who lost his drive in his later years and I don't want to see that happen to others."
4. "These animals are vital to their ecosystems and they cannot go extinct."

Step 5: Journal Everything that Comes to Mind.

Use free form. Get messy. Scratch things out. Draw pictures. Don't stop and analyze what you're writing. Put everything that comes to your mind on paper. The time for analyzing what you've written comes later.

It may take some time for you to come up with some concrete ideas. Again, that's fine. If you return home from your Mission-discovering session with nothing more than a bunch of scratched-out stuff on paper, that's okay. There is no rule that says you have to nail this on your first try.

Honestly, if you *do* think you get it on your first try,

you likely didn't dream big enough. Revisit it in a week or two and build on what you have.

Step 6: Let it Sit

Once you've pinpointed the specifics of your Mission, you should have something that's a mix of exciting and scary. Exciting, because it's something you could ideally see yourself working toward for the rest of your life. Scary, because you don't know how the hell you're going to pull off something so grand in scope.

The next step is to let go of it for a while. Let it percolate in the bottom of your brain for a few weeks. When you drop your Mission into the pressure cooker of your subconscious mind, your brain starts working on it whether you realize it or not. Don't be surprised when specific ideas for how to execute your life Mission begin popping up at seemingly random moments.

It's also fine to tweak your Mission over time. Maybe some aspects of it don't seem quite right after a few weeks or months. No problem—refine it. Maybe after a year you throw out the entire thing and start again. Also fine. Your Mission is a lifetime journey so it's worth getting right.

Additional Tips for Discovering Your Mission

Look to Your Childhood

Recall what you liked to do as a child or what you wanted to be when you grew up.

When we're young, our minds are open to all possibilities. The big bad world has not yet crushed our dreams. We are often in touch with what we're meant to do or be when we're young and then those dreams are forgotten as we age into other responsibilities and expectations.

Allow yourself to return to that simpler time. If you can't remember what you liked to do as a child or what you wanted to be, ask your parents.

Make Sure It's *Your* Mission

Don't copy another man's Mission.

You may have been one of those guys who emulated the head pastor, the youth pastor, the worship leader, or the missionary superstar in your church. You wanted to be just like them. Did that make you happy? No. It just led to comparisons, which will always bum you out.

One of the best things about uncovering your true Mission after you leave the Church is that you get to make it all about you. You can be as selfish as you want.

Keep Your Mission Private

Talking about your Mission to anyone and everyone opens yourself up to naysayers, doubters, and skeptics and you don't have time for that crap anymore. Since your Mission is deeply personal, most people won't understand it anyway, so why waste your breath trying to explain it? The few key people closest to you will understand and that's enough.

Also, as your Mission progresses, you may notice that some people want to join you. Be careful with this. If you open it up too much, you risk bringing in a bunch of value-suckers and wannabes—people who latch onto stronger men's Missions because they don't have one of their own and don't know how to create one. Help these guys find their own Mission rather than trying to bring them into yours.

It Doesn't Have to Be Noble

I realize that the Mission examples I gave above are impressively noble. But remember: It's okay to be selfish when you establish your Mission. Maybe you don't want to change the world for the better. Maybe your Mission is all about world travel, playing music, or surfing. That's okay!

Conclusion

For perhaps the first time in your life, you are developing a Mission and a reason to live *for you, by you*. Not the Church, not your parents, not your pastor, not your girlfriend, and not your friends.

For you, by you.

Once you have your Mission, you'll eventually start to grow into it. It will increasingly preoccupy your thoughts. You'll begin to develop specific action plans.

If you've discovered the right Mission for *you* (and no one else), you will end up on a trajectory that gives your life a new meaning outside the church. You will have a strong reason to get out of bed every morning. Other people will see the glow you carry around with you.

You will truly be born again.

Chapter 14
YOUR DECISION

"Knowing is not enough; we must apply. Willing is not enough; we must do." — Johann Wolfgang von Goethe

Several years ago, I had surgery on my shoulder. Afterward, the surgeon sent me to physical therapy.

On the first day of therapy, my newly repaired shoulder was stiff and painful. My physical therapist supervised me with some simple—yet difficult—exercises to slowly bring back the joint's function.

I hated having a bum shoulder. What made it worse is that I had injured my right side, which is my dominant side. I use that hand to write and do most things. I felt useless. I wanted to get my mobility back as soon as possible. So I did what my PT told me to do at every session. I did the assigned exercises at home religiously.

When I began to show improvement, I asked him if there were more advanced exercises I could do at home to hasten my recovery. He said he wasn't normally allowed to push patients faster, but he gave me some "under the table" movements I could "look forward to doing in a few weeks."

I took those and eased into them. It brought about my recovery even faster.

During my last session, while my PT was manipulating my shoulder as a final check, I looked around at his other patients. There were a lot of familiar faces in there by then—I had been going for several weeks. However, I noticed that some of these patients were still doing beginner exercises with small weights and a narrow range of motion.

"What's going on with them?" I asked my PT quietly. "They're still doing those, but they were coming here before I was."

He said something I'll never forget. "In here, recovery is ninety percent in the mind. You have to want to get better. If you believe you'll be injured for the rest of your life, then you will be. I see it every day."

"What do you do with the people who don't want to get better?" I asked.

He only shrugged. "There is nothing I can do. They have to want it first. Only after they make that decision can I help them."

Deconversion Is Painful and Difficult

Deconversion from your fundamentalist religion is like a devastating storm that tears through a town. Everyone in that town experiences some damage, but they are damaged in different ways. One person will have a tree fall on his roof. Another's house will flood. Still another will lose power for a week. Each of them has their own work to do to repair the damage and move on.

The fallout from deconversion will be different for everyone. Each of you will have your own unique journey of picking up the pieces.

There *will* be transitory pain. Expect it. View this pain as a force of resistance that is trying to put you back in line. It wants you to shut up and sit down. To obey. To get back on your knees before God. Some people do. But are they happy? Don't be one of them.

Comfort in Victimhood

Imagine yourself on a cold night wrapped in a warm blanket on a soft chair by a fire. You're reading a fantastic book or watching an engaging movie. Your pet is curled up beside you.

You're comfortable. You don't want to move from that environment. You don't want that comfort to end. But you know that eventually the comfort has to end. The fire will die out. The book or movie will end. The next day will come and you'll have to get up and go to work.

That's the thing about comfort. We want it to last but we know that it can't. Human beings can only find progress through overcoming obstacles and challenges, which is the precise antithetical definition of comfort.

This is not an easy thing to say, but there is a certain comfort in *victimhood*, in getting caught up in a cycle of thoughts that perpetuate this identity:

- The church did this to me!
- My pastor made me feel this way!
- The worship is manipulative!

What's difficult about feeling victimized is that it's *true*; you are *not wrong* to feel this way. But the other difficult truth about phrases of victimhood is that they do not serve your long-term goals. Eventually you will need to *make a decision* to fix what was damaged.

I get it. Sometimes it's easier to log onto an ex-Christian internet forum and vomit your complaints into a long thread. It feels good to receive sympathy. It feels even better when someone tells you they are going through the same thing. That makes you feel like you're not alone.

It's comfortable because you already know the alternative: Log off that forum, go out into the world, and face your rebuilding head on. But how do you get yourself in the right frame of mind to do that? You only need to ask yourself one question: "Will this kill me?"

The answer is obvious.

Do You Want to Get Better?

The reason I'll never forget what my PT told me that day was because he spoke wisdom that applied to all of life, not just physical therapy.

Throughout the years, I've met many people who don't want to get better. Whether it's a toxic relationship or a smoking habit or an anger issue, they simply have not decided once and for all to do something about it. Therefore, nothing will change no matter who tries to help them or how much they pray.

That's the sad truth about our world. Especially in this internet and technological age when the information and resources we need are only a click away. It's never been easier to find solutions to problems.

At the same time, the challenge of solving those problems is still the same. Getting better requires a commitment and a decision. It necessitates action. You can know everything there is to know about getting better, but in the end, all that matters is what you do.

Now that you've read this book, you have a useful resource and new insights for moving you through and beyond your painful deconversion. If I could somehow make this book force you to take positive steps forward in your life, I would. But I can't. That is up to you.

Take a long look at yourself in the mirror. Think about where you are now, where you've been, and where you would like to go.

Do you want to get better?

Make your decision. The time is now.

The Importance of Time and Its Management

In Chapter 6, I briefly mentioned how fundamentalists don't value time because they believe in eternity where time doesn't matter. You now live in a different world.

If you haven't already, commit to doing some deep contemplation about time and how valuable it is. When I first deconverted, I put this off because I was scared. It meant coming to terms with the fact that after I die, everything is done. There would be no eternity where my soul would live on.

When you turn 30, your 20s are gone and they're never coming back.

When you turn 40, your 30s are gone and they're never coming back.

When you turn 50, your 40s are gone and they're never coming back.

And when your life is over (and there's no guarantee you will have a long one), you won't be spending an eternity in a blissful heaven, gazing down at the earth, waiting for all your friends and loved ones to join you.

Time is your only nonrenewable resource. You can always make more money. You can always find more food. You can always buy more gadgets. But time that passes is gone forever. Your life—your time on this earth—is yours and yours alone. No one can tell you what to do with it or how to spend it.

If you're spending your valuable time caught up in old Church beliefs or habits that don't serve you, identify them, set clear goals to rectify them, and then get to work.

You should keep a healthy level of urgency simmering beneath the goals you've set for yourself. Don't relegate them to "someday." How many times have you said to yourself, "Oh, wow, it's Halloween already? It feels like New Year was yesterday."

Time passes fast. You simply cannot put off your future any longer when the Church has claimed so much of your past.

You know what you need to do.

You've made your decision to get better.

You've set the goals to get those things done.

You understand that knowledge means nothing without meaningful action.

You understand that time is passing and that once it has, it's gone forever.

Now go and do.

ABOUT THE AUTHOR

When not writing, Chase Austin can be found working out, enjoying beer and whiskey with friends, and traveling internationally.

For free articles every week, check out the blog:

www.thedeconvertedman.com

Follow on social media:

Facebook
https://www.facebook.com/deconvertedman

Twitter
https://twitter.com/deconverted_man

Instagram
https:/www.instagram.com/thedeconvertedman/

NOTES

6. Your Health

1. https://journals.sagepub.com/doi/abs/10.2466/pr0.94.3.839-844
2. www.sciencedirect.com/science/article/pii/S0301051105000736
3. https://www.amjmed.com/article/S0002-9343(08)00314-8/abstract
4. https://www.nhs.uk/conditions/contraception/miss-combined-pill/
5. https://www.medicalnewstoday.com/articles/322290#chances-of-pregnancy
6. https://www.webmd.com/healthy-aging/news/20110607/testosterone-decline-not-inevitable-with-age#1
7. https://pubmed.ncbi.nlm.nih.gov/11782267/
8. https://www.healthline.com/health/low-testosterone/boosting-food#tuna
9. https://pubmed.ncbi.nlm.nih.gov/21632481/
10. https://pubmed.ncbi.nlm.nih.gov/21744023/
11. https://pubmed.ncbi.nlm.nih.gov/20352370/
12. https://www.ncbi.nlm.nih.gov/pmc/articles/PMC3880087/
13. https://pubmed.ncbi.nlm.nih.gov/21154195/
14. www.sciencedirect.com/science/article/abs/pii/0031938492904539

10. Your Relationships With Women

1. Arnold Schwarzenegger, *Total Recall: My Unbelievably True Life Story* (Simon & Schuster 2012)

11. Your Spirituality

1. https://www.iep.utm.edu/ockham/#SH6a
2. Walter Isaacson, *Leonardo Da Vinci* (Simon & Schuster 2017)

13. Your Mission

1. https://pubmed.ncbi.nlm.nih.gov/24760141/

www.ingramcontent.com/pod-product-compliance
Lightning Source LLC
Chambersburg PA
CBHW031101080526
44587CB00011B/775